'Jim O'Neill challenges the lazy consensus and persuades us that the great swing to the East should be welcomed rather than resented by an anxious West. This is a book we all needed'
Sir Martin Sorrell, CEO, WPP

'There is no better guide to the new map of the economic world than Jim O'Neill'
Niall Ferguson, author of *The Ascent of Money* and *Civilization*

'A passionate riff on the subject. O'Neill's enthusiasm for the BRIC story stands out'
Financial Times

'Jim O'Neill is Goldman Sachs's rock star'
Business Week

'The top foreign-exchange economist anywhere in the world in the past decade'
Gavyn Davies, former BBC chairman

'The guru of Goldman Sachs has long been ahead of the curve'
Blake Hounshell, *Foreign Policy*

'Reveals the next stages in the progress of the non-Western economies which have come to dominate corporate life across the world'
Daily Telegraph

'O'Neill encourages us to concentrate on the basics: population and productivity. It's the demography, stupid. Admirably simple'
Bloomberg Businessweek

'In four letters, Jim O'Neill identified one of the most consequential themes of the twenty-first century. Jim has changed how the world thinks about economic growth – and how the BRICs think about themselves'
Lloyd Blankfein, Chairman and CEO, Goldman Sachs

...ful analysis of the dynamic forces that are
...orld and the lives of millions of people.
...has done more than anyone to illuminate
the shifting landscape of the global economy'
Michael Spence, Nobel Prize-winning economist

'If you want to learn how emerging markets are going to develop
in the coming years, you don't have to wait for some future
historian: just read this wonderful book'
Arminio Fraga, economist and former President of
the Central Bank of Brazil

'Jim O'Neill's theory about the BRICs has become a reality.
His new book makes it clear that growth markets
will grow to the benefit of all'
Arkady Dvorkovich, advisor to Russian President
Dmitry Medvedev

'Compulsory reading for all those interested in the
world economy'
Montek Singh Ahluwalia, economist and Deputy Chairman
of the Planning Commission of the Republic of India

'Jim O'Neill's book provides us with more insights into
how the world is better with BRICs emerging. Just like
the book says, it is a great challenge indeed, but it is
a great opportunity worth exploring'
Professor FAN Gang, Director of NERI-China (National
Economic Research Institute, China Reform Foundation)

ABOUT THE AUTHOR

Jim O'Neill is Chairman of Goldman Sachs Asset Management. He
joined Goldman Sachs in 1995, rising to chief economist, and in 2001 he
led the team that conducted the original BRIC analysis. He is a member
of the boards of the UK Royal Economic Society, Itinera and Bruegel,
and also chairman of the charity SHINE. He has a lifelong passion for
Manchester United FC, and has served as a non-executive director of
the club's board.

JIM O'NEILL

The Growth Map

*Economic Opportunity in
the BRICs and Beyond*

PORTFOLIO
PENGUIN

PORTFOLIO PENGUIN

Published by the Penguin Group
Penguin Books Ltd, 80 Strand, London WC2R 0RL, England
Penguin Group (USA) Inc., 375 Hudson Street, New York, New York 10014, USA
Penguin Group (Canada), 90 Eglinton Avenue East, Suite 700, Toronto, Ontario, Canada M4P 2Y3
(a division of Pearson Penguin Canada Inc.)
Penguin Ireland, 25 St Stephen's Green, Dublin 2, Ireland (a division of Penguin Books Ltd)
Penguin Group (Australia), 707 Collins Street, Melbourne, Victoria 3008, Australia
(a division of Pearson Australia Group Pty Ltd)
Penguin Books India Pvt Ltd, 11 Community Centre,
Panchsheel Park, New Delhi – 110 017, India
Penguin Group (NZ), 67 Apollo Drive, Rosedale, Auckland 0632, New Zealand
(a division of Pearson New Zealand Ltd)
Penguin Books (South Africa) (Pty) Ltd, Block D, Rosebank Office Park,
181 Jan Smuts Avenue, Parktown North, Gauteng 2193, South Africa

Penguin Books Ltd, Registered Offices: 80 Strand, London WC2R 0RL, England

www.penguin.com

First published 2011
This edition published 2013
001

Set in 10.68/13pt Sabon LT Std
Typeset by Jouve (UK), Milton Keynes
Printed in Great Britain by Clays Ltd, St Ives plc

ISBN: 978-0-241-95807-0

www.greenpenguin.co.uk

ALWAYS LEARNING   **PEARSON**

To my family

Contents

Introduction: Audacious Growth

In the spring of 2008 I booked a surprise twenty-fifth wedding anniversary present for my wife. We were to go trekking to the base camp of Everest in the Himalayas. I had booked the trip for October. Three weeks before we were due to leave, Lehman Brothers, the fourth largest bank in the USA, declared itself bankrupt, triggering a global financial crisis.

At the time I was still the chief economist at the London office of Goldman Sachs, another leading US investment bank. I was torn. Should I go ahead with the trip, which would take me not only out of the office for fourteen days, but also out of contact? From the perspective of the financial industry the world seemed to be falling apart. After much deliberation, I decided we should still go. If I waited for the world to be without a crisis, I might never take a holiday. And I needed the break. Over the previous weeks I had been working non-stop, including every weekend. Staying in the office would not solve the crisis. Rather, getting away might give me time to reflect, far from all the noise.

On our way to Mount Everest we spent a night in the Nepalese capital Kathmandu, awaiting the hair-raising flight to Lukla's Tenzing-Hillary airport. We were the only diners in our hotel's restaurant, so the maître d' had time to chat to us through dinner. At one point he mentioned the 'credit crisis' sweeping the globe. To those of us in the West the credit crisis was about the sudden unavailability of loans. But in Nepal, where so much commerce is conducted in cash or barter, this was irrelevant. What concerned our talkative maître d' was the relentless rise in energy costs. Sub-prime mortgage defaults may have been of no interest in Kathmandu, but fuel prices definitely were.

As he spoke, it occurred to me that what mattered to him was almost certainly what mattered to the people of China and India. Provided the price of oil fell back to its previous level, this crisis we all thought of as 'global' would not be global at all, but merely Western. I owe that maître d' a large drink for sparking this insight.

As we embarked on our trip to Everest Base Camp, we came to a small town called Namche Bazaar, perched on the edge of a plateau some 3,800 metres above sea level. Its market serves Everest's many climbing parties and all the local trading communities. Tibetan merchants lead their yaks and donkeys over the high, treacherous mountains to bring their wares for sale. I had read about these adventurous traders, though I'd found the stories difficult to believe. But I discovered that, not only did they make the long and arduous trek to Namche Bazaar, they also exchanged information about market conditions on the way using mobile telephones. I was amazed: they were calling each other on a Chinese network from halfway up a Himalayan mountain while I couldn't even get a signal in some remote parts of the UK.

One of the very last newspaper articles I had read before I left London had been claiming globalization was finished. Yet here before us, high in the Himalaya, I could see one of the greatest modern tools of trade being used by men who at first sight might be described as primitive. Here was a powerful example of how globalization was alive and well. It occurred to me then how narrowly focused many of us can be.

In 2001 I wrote a research paper in Goldman Sachs' Global Economics series that examined the relationship between the world's leading economies and some of the larger emerging market economies.[1]

I thought the global economy in the coming decades would be propelled by the growth of four populous and economically ambitious countries: Brazil, Russia, India and China, and I coined the acronym BRIC from their initials to describe them.

Since then my career has been shaped in large part by that single term. Even then I had stopped thinking of these four economies as traditional emerging markets. Ten years later I am even more eager to convince the world that they, along with some other rising stars, are the growth engines of the world economy, today and in the future.

When the credit crisis erupted in September 2008 many predicted that the BRIC story was over. There were moments I worried about that too. In the immediate aftermath, BRIC equity markets fell more than those of their developed cousins and it did seem as though global trade might suffer permanent scars. Of course, this fear turned out to be completely unfounded. In some ways that is when the BRIC thesis really came of age. It withstood the shakings of the world's economic foundations, and emerged more robust than ever.

My paper did not cause an immediate splash and its main points were not seen as especially profound at the time. Based on my analysis of global GDP, I wrote that four countries, Brazil, Russia, India and China, which then controlled

8 per cent of the world GDP, would see their share of the world economy grow significantly in the next decade. I noted that China's GDP was already bigger than that of Italy, which was a well-entrenched member of the G7 group of economic superpowers, and over the decade ahead it would start to overtake a number of the other G7 members. Over the next ten years, I predicted that the weight of the BRICs – and especially China – in world GDP would grow quite markedly. The world would have to pay attention.

I predicted that Brazil, given highly favourable but what then appeared to be very unlikely conditions, could by 2011 increase its GDP to 'not far behind Italy'. Brazil's GDP overtook Italy's in 2010, making it the seventh largest economy in the world, with a GDP of around $2.1 trillion.

The other three BRICs have made similarly impressive progress. In the first two months of 2011, for example, we learned that China's economy had overtaken Japan's as the world's second largest; IndiGO, a little-known low-cost Indian airline, had ordered 180 A320s, making it two-thirds the size of Europe's long-established easyJet; and Russia had become Europe's largest car sales market.

All four of the BRIC countries have exceeded the expectations I had of them back in 2001. Looking back, those earliest predictions, shocking to some at the time, now seem rather conservative. The aggregate GDP of the BRIC countries has close to quadrupled since 2001, from around $3 trillion to between $11 and $12 trillion. The world economy has doubled in size since 2001, and a third of that growth has come from the BRICs. Their combined GDP increase was more than twice that of the United States and it was equivalent to the creation of another new Japan plus one Germany, or five United Kingdoms, in the space of a single decade.

Some observers say the effect of the BRICs on the world economy has been exaggerated because their growth was primarily driven by exports to the developed markets, as well as the rise in commodity prices. Exports certainly played a major role for China, but since the 2008 credit crisis and the consequent fall in demand in the US and elsewhere, that is no longer the case. For India, domestic demand has been the driver throughout the last decade, and increasingly it is the domestic consumer as well as an increase in infrastructure spending that is fuelling growth in the BRIC economies. The credit-fuelled growth in US demand certainly played its part in their ascent, but even since 2008, and despite the ongoing US struggles, the BRIC economies have continued to power ahead.

However you choose to interpret the data, the importance of the BRICs in global economic growth is beyond dispute. Personal consumption in the BRIC countries has skyrocketed. In China, between 2001 and 2010, domestic spending increased by $1.5 trillion, or roughly the size of the UK economy. The increase in the other three was about the same, perhaps slightly more. BRICs now account for probably close to 20 per cent of world trade compared to less than 10 per cent in 2001. Trade between the BRICs has risen far more quickly than global trade as a whole.

Given the BRICs' success, it should be no surprise that many other countries are now vying to be dubbed the next BRIC. Friends from Indonesia goad me whenever I see them, suggesting that BRIC should really have been BRICI. Mexican policymakers tell me it should have been BRICM. In Turkey they wish it had been BRICT.

In 2003 my Goldman Sachs colleagues Dominic Wilson and Roopa Purushothaman published a follow-up paper,

'Dreaming with BRICs: The Path to 2050', extending my earlier analysis to the middle of the century.[2] They wrote that, by 2035, China could overtake the US to become the largest economy in the world, and by 2039 the combined GDP of the BRIC economies could become bigger than that of the G7.

That paper started to command the attention of many, even though most thought it fanciful at the time. But our updated research suggests that it was anything but: China's economic output – its gross domestic product – could match that of the US as early as 2027, and perhaps even sooner. Since 2001 China's GDP has risen fourfold, from $1.5 trillion to $6 trillion. Economically speaking, China has created three new Chinas in the past decade. And it's likely that the combined GDP of the four BRIC nations will exceed that of the US sometime before 2020.

In 2005, my team at Goldman Sachs tried to determine which would be the next group of developing countries to follow in the BRICs' wake. We came up with a group that we called the 'Next Eleven', or N-11 for short. They are Bangladesh, Egypt, Indonesia, Iran, (South) Korea, Mexico, Nigeria, Pakistan, the Philippines, Turkey and Vietnam. Although we thought no N-11 country was likely to grow to the size of any of the BRICs, we predicted that Mexico and Korea had the capacity to become almost as important as the BRICs in the global economy.[3]

As with the BRICs, I was surprised at how quickly and widely the N-11 concept was embraced. It has become an important framework used by many, from investors to global policymakers, to interpret the changes in the global economy. Such frameworks have become more useful than ever, given the speed and magnitude of these changes. The BRICs and the N-11 don't explain everything, but they have proved useful and enduring models to help our understanding of what is happening in the world's economy and markets.

In early 2011 I decided that the term 'emerging markets' could no longer be applied to the BRICs and four of the N-11: Indonesia, Korea, Mexico and Turkey. These are now countries with largely sound government debt and deficit positions, robust trading networks and huge numbers of people all moving steadily up the economic ladder. For investors to understand the scale of the opportunity here, and for policymakers to grasp what is changing in the world, they must see these countries apart from the traditional 'emerging markets'. I decided that a more accurate term would be Growth Markets.

The popularity of such easy categorization, however, should be a warning in itself. In 1977, when I was coming to the end of my Masters degree in Economics and Finance, my supervisor suggested that I should consider studying for a PhD in Economics. He said that a grant could be available at the University of Surrey in the Energy Economics centre. I decided to take up the offer at what proved to be an exciting time.

It was 1979 and the revolution in Iran had just provoked a second oil crisis, so applying the monetary economics I had studied to the world of OPEC's oil producers and their investments seemed interesting. I spent the next two years delving into theories around oil prices, cartels and international asset allocation. I often joke to fellow economists that perhaps the only thing I learned from my PhD was how to keep my sanity. The endless hours and days sitting alone in a computer room or the library trying to find the definitive answer to how OPEC should invest its surpluses was challenging. But the work forced me to realize that economics is a social science. There are no certainties in economics. What passes for common wisdom is often no more than a lazy consensus, overconfidence in the face of inordinate complexity.

It was common wisdom in the late 1970s and early 1980s that crude oil prices would rise far into the future. Yet by the mid-1980s oil prices had fallen. This trend continued for much of the next two decades. Consensus thinking, even among highly trained economists, misunderstood the responsiveness of supply and demand to the rise in oil prices. In the short term, oil suppliers and consumers are slow to respond to spikes in prices. But over the long term they have proved to be much more flexible than economists generally believed they would. I will return to this subject later in the context of China's prodigious energy demands, but I mention it now to illustrate how frequently economists are wrong. The lazy consensus is a powerful, smothering force. And attempting to identify it and challenge it is something we all should do.

Technology is driving a dramatic new phase of globalization. Our economic models struggle to keep pace with the erosion of national economic borders. There have also been extraordinary political changes of late. China and Russia closed themselves off from the rest of the world in terms of Western ideas and economic policies following the Second World War, but today 1.3 billion people in China and 140 million Russians are being allowed to live their lives in much the same manner as any Westerner, and are making many of the same consumer choices. Even under their own very different political systems, it is evident that they too crave the fruits of rising individual wealth.

Manchester United Football Club, which I have followed passionately since I was a boy, reportedly has 70 million registered subscribers to its website in China. McDonald's has thriving restaurants throughout China and Russia. Fashionable clothing stores are on the rise in both. The French luxury goods company Louis Vuitton is seeing explosive growth in China and the other BRIC countries. Even its Western stores are now selling briskly to tourists from these nations.

Indeed, French students can now make a small personal 'turn' as guest shoppers for luxury bags at Louis Vuitton's landmark Parisian store just off the Champs-Élysées. The head of Louis Vuitton told me how this works. Chinese gangs used to pay people to go on two-day all-expenses-paid trips to Paris on the condition that they returned with four Louis Vuitton bags, which could then be sold at a mark-up in China. When Louis Vuitton found out, it introduced a limit of one bag per person. To get round the limit, Chinese visitors now offer likely looking individuals on the Champs-Élysées $50 to purchase a bag on their behalf.

China's deliberate decision to embrace globalization for its own gain by encouraging foreign direct investment and a greater participation in world trade has, I believe, prompted India into action. While there are many factors which lead to economic growth, I am convinced that China's success over the past thirty years taught India's policymakers that it is possible for more than a billion people to experience a dramatic increase in their living standards without changing their basic social and cultural structure.

By deciding they wanted to engage more in the world economy, the BRICs also became open to the best of the West's macroeconomic policies. Their politicians and academics suddenly wanted to learn and apply the lessons of Western growth.

In Brazil, for example, the decision to target the hyperinflation which had ravaged the country's economy for decades proved transformational. The adoption and disciplined enforcement of anti-inflationary measures helped to put the Brazil of 2000 on a very different course from the Brazil of 1960.

The ascent and continued success of Brazil, Russia, India and China has surprised many – myself included. It is a phenomenon that has begun to transform the lives of millions of people in these nations, lifting them out of poverty and revolutionizing their ambitions, and is increasingly touching us all. The BRIC concept, the rapid advance of these economies and the rosy prospects for others like them has become the dominant story of our generation.

I

The Birth of the BRICs

The idea had begun to form in my mind two months earlier. I had been in New York to address the National Association of Business Economists at the Marriott Hotel in the World Trade Center. The title of my speech was 'The Outlook for the Dollar' and I drew heavily on my life as a foreign exchange economist. Not once did I mention the BRICs. In fact, at that time the only BRIC economy I gave much thought to was China. Two days later I was back in London, tired from the three-day trip back and forth across the Atlantic. At the time I was co-head of the Global Economics department at Goldman Sachs. It was early afternoon and I was taking part in an audio/video conference with our senior economists from all over the world. It was the best of globalization in action, diverse voices and opinions pouring in from New York, Tokyo and Hong Kong, with us pitching in from London.

My mind was taken up with the imminent departure of my co-head Gavyn Davies, one of the most respected economists in the world. He left the meeting early for his final interview for the post of chairman of the BBC. A short while later he was back, with news that an aeroplane had struck the Twin Towers. Failing to appreciate the full extent of what was happening, we carried on with our meeting. A couple of minutes later our New York colleagues rose and disappeared from the video screen without explanation.

We all know what happened next in Lower Manhattan. Over the next few days I received emails from friends and colleagues I had seen so recently in New York, people who had heard me speak at the conference, people I scarcely knew offering up their extraordinary tales of escape from the terror and turmoil of that awful morning. Some, in their confusion, were still asking for copies of the charts I had shown to explain my views on the dollar.

The same technology that had given us the ability to talk so easily to colleagues around the world could also convey the horrific reality of the devastation the terrorists caused. We could watch the Towers burning and collapsing in real time. It was a chilling example of the immediacy of advanced technology and communication, its ability to strike a collective fear into the whole world. The nature of the media was clearly understood by the terrorists, too.

The 9/11 attacks unleashed a cascade of thoughts which had been building in my own mind as my career progressed. They were linked to the pros and cons of globalization. I wondered whether there were better ways to think about economic growth around the world, some idea that could be shared and accepted by everyone, and which would transcend nationalism.

Globalization, I felt, had come to be equated with Americanization, which was not always welcome in every part of the world. And yet the benefits of globalization – if only they could be understood on their own, without seeming to belong to any one country, culture or political system – seemed obvious. A more open exchange of goods, services, currencies, and even political influence, could lead to greater wealth for all, not just the elites.

Over the next couple of weeks, as people tried to recover a semblance of normality, Gavyn accepted the post of BBC Chairman, and I was asked to assume sole leadership of the Global Economics department. It was a great honour, but also a great challenge. Gavyn had built the department into a world-class research group. His team had come to be regarded as masters of sophisticated and detailed analyses of the largest economies, especially the G7. How could I ever take over his mantle and maintain the department's reputation?

A brief personal history might explain the reason for my apprehension. Until I joined Goldman Sachs in 1995, I had spent most of my years as a 'dirty economist', someone who mixed classical economics with the rough and tumble of the trading floor. My speciality was foreign exchange. I had fallen into the field in 1982, after my doctorate at the University of Surrey. I needed a well-paid job because I had borrowed so much during my education and so I gravitated to the City of London. The traditional British clearing banks would have been an unlikely home for me, because I hadn't been to the top schools or Oxbridge. In those days, such things still mattered more. The bank which did offer me a job was Bank of America. I confess I was naïve: because the name was so similar to the Bank of England, I'd originally thought it was the London branch of the US Federal Reserve rather than a multinational corporation. But the bank gave me a chance and I was grateful for it.

At Bank of America there were still strong traces of academic economics, which could reach the level of the absurd. The first country I was asked to analyse was Italy. Once a month I had a conference call with economists in the bank's headquarters in San Francisco, to discuss the five-year out-look for the lira. The currency was so volatile that often we didn't actually know where it was trading on the day, never mind in the future. After a few of these meetings, I could tell you to the minute when someone would predict that Italy would soon default. Its debt/GDP ratio at the time was roughly where it is today: well over 100 per cent. The fact that Italy kept stumbling along, and was not even close to default, suggested to me that finance was full of people claim-ing to know far more than they did.

I subsequently moved to Marine Midland in London and then in 1985 on to New York with the same firm. I loved New York. The meritocracy of the place suited me, the way the thing that mattered most was whether you were capable and if what you had to say made sense. As a trading-floor economist, which is what I was when I went to New York, I was spending time in the noisy world of foreign exchange traders and I learned from some of the most aggressive and talented of them.

Part of my job entailed me waiting for the telex machine to start printing. I would grab the latest news and interpret it. If the Bundesbank raised interest rates, what did it mean for the dollar/Deutschmark rate? How could the traders use this news? I had to make my formal training more immediately relevant.

The experience of watching the volumes and liquidity of the foreign exchange market made me realize that it's like the world's biggest fruit and vegetable store. Everyone knows everything all the time. There is no secrecy about the quality of the goods or what their prices ought to be. You can trade the euro/dollar exchange from 8 p.m. on Sunday night to 10 p.m. on Friday. There's no other market like it, and if you want to make money, you are forced to take agile and some-times contrary views. You have to ask yourself if other investors are in there too early or too late. You've got to be constantly on your guard against the lazy consensus, because one shift in a market that is so big and liquid, where there's so much information, and you can easily get caught out.

Trying to be permanently smart in this market is tough. It's why it tends to attract larger-than-life characters, people who are ready to take big, risky positions, with the possibility of great gain or loss. Only they can buck the powerful group-think in foreign exchange trading. (In this regard, fast forward to spring 2010, when I was chairing a discussion at a Gold-man Sachs conference of chief investment officers. It was just as the European crisis surrounding Greece broke out and I asked the question: 'Who thinks the euro is going to be stronger against the dollar by the end of the year?' Two people raised their hands. Then I asked: 'Who thinks it's going to be weaker?' Everyone else raised their hands. Of course, by the end of the year, the euro was a lot stronger. Experiences like these shaped how I think as an economist trying to make sense of the world.)

In 1988 I joined the Swiss Bank Corporation (SBC), work-ing in fixed income and equity markets. Within a year I was running the bank's global research network, learning about equities as I went. I realized that my job as head of a research unit, aside from managing people, was to come up with just a few interesting ideas to communicate both inside and outside the bank. I was encouraged to think about the potential growth of a bond market to serve the European Community, as the European Union was then called, perhaps because I was sur-rounded by several continental colleagues who seemed very absorbed by the idea of European Monetary Union (EMU).

At the time the idea of a single currency was still very much in the planning stage, but I was persuaded that the process was unstoppable, and that inevitably the various European domestic bond markets would adapt to this new reality. In fact, it had been possible to buy bonds denominated in this as-yet unadopted common currency since 1981. What would become the euro was then known as the European currency unit, or ECU. In 1990 I created a model to track ECU bond trading, which, although idiotically simplistic, helped brand SBC as a credible player in this market.

EMU turned out to be a good learning process for me, in terms of focusing on the big picture. I had already learned a lot about the various major European currencies from my Marine Midland days. Many traders I knew specialized in just a couple of trades, for example the yen against the lira. The volatility of Italy's currency meant there were always ample opportunities for both making and losing money, and many traders shed a tear for its passing. The arrival of the euro forced the foreign exchange world to seek out new opportunities, to cast our gaze around the world.

Coincidentally 1990, the year I developed the ECU bond model, was also the first year I visited China. I've been at least once a year every year since then, at first to talk to the people who managed foreign exchange reserves at the Bank of China (some of whom became good friends). I didn't realize it at the time, but those early visits were paving the way for the story that would later dominate my professional life.

In the early 1990s I joined the growing crowd of economists who believed the US dollar had to weaken. I expected that the dollar would fall sharply against the Japanese yen. I did not think the US could cope with its external balance without letting its currency devalue. I was proved right, and this call on the US dollar/yen is what probably made me more widely known in the investment banking world and among hedge funds. By the mid-1990s I had joined Goldman Sachs as a partner. Once there I was constantly seeking ways to prove myself worthy of my place among the best team of economists at any major bank, casting around for ideas.

I had come to look forward to my regular visits to China and could see the changes every time I went. But the event that transformed my view of China was the 1997 Asian economic crisis, when the value of currencies throughout the region collapsed. My interpretation of the crisis was that while excessive borrowing by many Asian countries might have been the core cause, equally significant was the reversal of the yen's strength in mid-1995. When it started to become clear that Japan would struggle to recover from the bursting of its asset bubble, and that interest rates would stay really low in Japan, the yen weakened notably through 1996 and 1997. For many other Asian countries whose currencies were linked to the dollar, this represented quite a problem. From 1973 to 1997, the yen had risen from ¥400 to ¥80 against the dollar, and Asia probably believed that the yen would continue to rise for ever. When it started to weaken, as it did in mid-1995, it began to expose all the Asian countries and companies which had borrowed huge amounts in dollars. As long as the yen was rising, their debts were manageable and shrinking, as they could pay off their dollar debt with the yen they received from exporting goods to the Japanese; the moment the yen weakened the cost of servicing and paying down that dollar debt began to rise. In addition, as the dollar rose against the yen, the price of these countries' exports rose, and Japanese investors were less attracted to these countries. Starting with the Thai baht, currencies across Asia began to tumble.

If history was any guide, the crisis should have clicked its way through the various Asian countries and finally caused utter chaos in China. Instead, the Chinese demonstrated the kind of astuteness and global awareness I hadn't seen before. They appeared to think that in order to avoid contagion from the crisis, they would have to take a global view and role rather than local ones.

Since the root of the problem was the relationship between the dollar and the yen, the Chinese called the White House and told the Americans they had to intervene. They even threatened to devalue their own currency, the renminbi (also called the yuan), if the Americans resisted, which would probably have escalated the crisis even more. Supporting the yen would be against the stated US policy in favour of a strong dollar, but President Clinton and his treasury secretary, Bob Rubin, listened and began buying the yen. It worked. The contagion was stopped, and China had demonstrated that it possessed economic brains and growing political brawn. Some argue about the impact of US intervention and say that other factors took the heat out of the Asian crisis by strengthening the yen. But in my book, the Chinese had played an important global role and persuaded the Americans to support their position. I for one was impressed.

That started me thinking about how the structure of the world economy was changing and what that would mean for certain developmental and policy issues. As an economist specializing in foreign exchange markets, I had grown up with the G5 and G7 playing the defining role in global economic policy.[1] In 1985 the original 'Group of Five' – the United States, Japan, France, West Germany and the United Kingdom – had gathered at the Plaza Hotel in New York to sign the Plaza Accord, agreeing to intervene in currency markets to depreciate the value of the dollar in relation to the yen and the Deutschmark. In 1987 those five countries plus Canada and Italy, the G7, had conspired again, this time at the Louvre in Paris, to try to halt the decline in the dollar they had triggered two years earlier. These two events had a major impact on my career and how I thought about markets, and economic policy. The world's economic policy at the time was shaped by a small group of people from a handful of countries meeting in luxury hotels and grand museums. One of my mantras for successfully analysing the foreign exchange markets became 'Never ignore the G7'. They seemed so powerful, and when they were determined, very successful.

The creation of the European Monetary Union, and the merging of so many currencies into a single one, had already made clear to me that the G7 had outlived its usefulness. If Germany, France and Italy now had a single monetary policy and currency, what was the point of each of them showing up at G7 meetings? A single representative would suffice. In addition, extrapolation of growth patterns of the late 1990s (and China's ability to withstand the strains of the Asian currency crisis) showed that, not long after the millennium, China would overtake Italy in terms of GDP, and soon afterwards be up there with France, the UK and Germany.

The case for reform of the G7 was obvious back then; it is quite remarkable that it took the US until 2008 to lead the revival of the G20, an already existing though moribund grouping comprising nineteen major countries plus the European Union, which was the first real step down this path.[2]

In 2001, what particularly interested me about Brazil, Russia, India and China was that they all appeared increasingly eager to engage on the global stage. Whatever had occurred in their past was over and done with. Globalization was happening and they wanted to be part of it. The internet was obviously helping, enabling companies to outsource more and more activities to cheaper parts of the world. China was an easy pick, given its size and the enthusiasm of its leaders to embrace capitalism – or at least large parts of it. What also intrigued me was that the more I visited these countries, and the more dealings I had with the senior officials and their underlings over many years, the more I realized that they were equally well-informed about the world as I was. If those billion-plus people had access to the same technology and advantages enjoyed in the West, their progress would be prodigious.

There were other unique economic factors which determined the BRICs' status as countries to watch. India's demographics were so powerful and the fact that so many Indians spoke English put them in a great position to benefit from the internet, and the boom in outsourcing services. Here was another nation of more than 1 billion people that seemed to want to embrace globalization and to allow its workforce and products to enter the global marketplace. I thought that this could be the start of a whole new era for India. Lots of smart Indian business people could bring international business to Indians, and the benefits of India to the rest of the world.

Russia had already been invited to join the G7 in 1997 as the West sought to encourage the country towards free markets and democracy following the collapse of communism. By 2001 the G7 leaders had given up on Russia to a degree. The replacement of Boris Yeltsin by Vladimir Putin had slowed Russia's progress towards capitalism, to the disappointment of the West. This mindset lies at the heart of why some Western observers today find it so easy to be sceptical about Russia. As I will discuss later, Russia can still generate the economic might and opportunities that the G7 perceived back in the 1990s. However, it may just be delivered in a different style from that expected by the G7 when they became the G8.

The case for China, India and Russia was obvious, but I was trying to think globally and wondered if I were missing something. I hadn't really thought that closely about Latin America but there were two countries there with large populations: Brazil and Mexico. Brazil seemed an increasingly likely candidate because, like China during the Asian crisis, it had recently become a more thoughtful economic player. Around this same time, Argentina had broken the link between its currency and the dollar and defaulted, seemingly joining much of the rest of the continent in economic struggle.

There were signs that Brazil was starting to go in a different direction, and not a moment too soon. Brazil had been a democracy since the early 1980s, but it had always struggled to achieve the stability essential for making serious economic progress. The problems of corruption and inefficiency were endemic. For ordinary people that manifested itself in daily life with prices so volatile it was impossible to predict how much anything would cost. One of Goldman Sachs' own Brazilian economists told me that when he was a teenager, Brazilian inflation on a daily basis was what it is today on an annual basis. In my professional lifetime, Brazil has had four different currencies, a reflection of the economic chaos which has plagued the country. In the 1990s alone Brazil went through three financial crises. For years, any rich Brazilian converted their money and shoved it out to Switzerland as quickly as they could, before it became worthless.

This all changed in the late 1990s, when a new set of political leaders, led by President Fernando Cardoso, set about bringing inflation under control and improving the country's fiscal health. I strongly believe that taming inflation is essential for any economy to grow on a sustainable basis. People need to know what their money will buy. If they can't trust prices, they won't invest or do anything to improve their future. Without giving people the sense that whatever they earn and save is going to have value, no politician can talk seriously about sustained growth. If I could recommend only one policy to any country hoping to join in the success of the developed world, it would be this: target inflation and hold it down. Brazil's opportunity came in the brief period after 1999, following yet another economic crisis. Brazil's leaders floated the real, letting it promptly drop in value, and appointed Arminio Fraga, a fan of inflation targeting, as the new head of the central bank. By placing the control of inflation at the centre of macroeconomic policy, it at last seemed that Brazil's leaders had the will to end the hyperinflation cycles of the previous two decades, and give their country a serious chance to reach its potential.

But with so many unknowns, the inclusion of Brazil was undoubtedly the biggest, boldest bet I took when I wrote my 2001 paper. I can't resist saying, in the spirit of the amusing debate back in those days about why I included the B in BRICs, that Brazil also happens to produce some of the world's best football players (an ongoing subject of obsession for this author).

So I arrived at the point of creating an economic grouping and realized that, by taking the initial capitals of the names of these four nations, I could make an acronym that was particularly apposite, for these four BRICs, with a total population of around 2.8 billion, might indeed be the new 'bricks' from which the modern economy would be built. The 9/11 attacks had forced my collection of observations into a coherent form. Perhaps if I could envisage and, indeed, contribute to a world in which there was no unequivocally 'right' way and no 'accepted' leading nation – one in which we all tolerated each other under some commonly agreed international principles of conduct – then this world could be a better and safer place.

Globalization didn't need to be Americanization; there was scope for the rest of the world to create their own definition of the term using their own characteristics. Even today there are Americans who seem to feel that allowing China to grow as big as the United States would represent a challenge to everything America stands for. In 2001 that attitude was rife. I wanted to put a stop to this kind of thinking: to help people see globalization as benefiting everyone. This is what inspired the November 2001 paper and what has greatly influenced me ever since. In this book I will outline how these four nations have progressed far beyond even my own expectations, how their actions have encouraged and inspired other emerging nations to join the global economy, how they are helping the post-2008-crisis West recover its economic health, and why they will be crucial to a better economic future for us all.

2

From Emerging to Emerged

It is striking how much has changed in just a decade, but also how little the original BRICs' framework has altered. In all my analysis of world economies, amid all the information and hype, I have stayed focused on the benefits of an expanding, more productive workforce. While the 2001 paper turned out to be the beginning of years of research and analysis on those themes, and my colleagues and I have subsequently refined them, the framework itself has stayed the same.

The BRICs have outperformed even our most optimistic scenarios and we have revised the paths first set out to 2050 on three occasions. The aggregate GDP of the BRIC countries quadrupled during the decade following my original paper, from $3 trillion to close to $12 trillion. In hindsight I should have been even bolder in my predictions.

Even though I had always known it from my basic economics training, I had not fully appreciated the simple but critical importance of demographics and productivity. In this chapter I lay out how we thought about both these factors as the BRIC story started to become more influential.

THE POWER OF DEMOGRAPHICS

I wasn't the only one who didn't pay enough attention to demographics. In European business and policymaking circles, I often hear people talking enviously about growth in the United States versus Europe, or with astonishment at the growth in India and China. A lot of it is due to the demographics. Simply applying the most credible estimates of long-term demographic trends, especially for the working population, is the intellectual cornerstone of the argument for the BRICs' potential.

Between them, the four BRIC countries are home to close on 3 billion people, not far off half the world's population. In some ways, it shouldn't be that much of a surprise that anyone should think they would be the potentially largest economies. The world's largest populated nations probably should have the biggest economies. Certainly, in order for their people to enjoy the wealth that many throughout the rest of the world enjoy, they would need to have big successful economies. As the late Angus Maddison (a recognized expert on the history and analysis of economic growth and development) has shown, the two most populous countries, China and India, in the past constituted a much bigger share of global GDP. In his pathbreaking analysis of economic history, Maddison showed that China dominated the world between the tenth and fifteenth centuries in terms of both size and wealth.[1] For centuries until then, India was the dominant economy and, at times, the two countries' combined share of global GDP was above 50 per cent.

Why couldn't it happen again? I believe it will.

*

Of course, the four countries are very different. Not all of them will necessarily succeed. China and India are the two huge nations, with populations more than four times the size of the US. If China and India's working population could ever be as productive individually as America's, then in simple terms they would be four times bigger economically. Brazil and Russia have much smaller populations than China and India, with around 180 million and 140 million respectively, but this is more than any country in Europe, and indeed more than the 125 million or so population of Japan. In its most simple sense, this means that they could be bigger economies.

When I was studying Geography and Economics at university in the mid-1970s, the US had a population of around 200 million. Today it is 300 million. This fact alone goes a good way towards explaining why the US has grown so much more than Europe. More working people make an economy easier to grow, unless of course they are extremely unproductive (as can be the case in many developing economies). More people produce more output. More people earn wages and income, which is the basis for their consumption. This is a pretty straightforward fact of economic life – and one that is essential to consider when thinking about the BRICs.

THE POWER OF PRODUCTIVITY

The other essential driver of growth is productivity. The more a group of workers can produce with a given set of inputs, from time to materials, the faster their economy will grow. Assuming that workers in developed countries are already highly productive, for reasons ranging from more advanced technology to better infrastructure and health care, workers in less developed countries have a lot more opportunity to catch them up if they can fulfil their potential.

The scale of the opportunity for productivity growth is much larger in developing countries than in developed ones. The economics profession frequently complicates this fact, but it really is this straightforward. Countries with young and expanding labour forces, which are becoming increasingly efficient, will show the largest gains in real GDP. The major reason the United States outperformed Europe economically from 1980 to 2010 was that it had more people entering the workforce and working longer hours. Americans were not dramatically more productive; there were just more of them working harder. As I looked at the BRICs, it seemed likely that a similar pattern would emerge in these four countries, on an even more dramatic scale.

In the November 2001 paper, I showed via simple extrapolation that as soon as 2010 the combined GDP of the four BRIC countries was likely to become a bigger share of the world's GDP under almost any assumptions. I presented four different scenarios for how the decade could evolve and demonstrated how the BRICs' combined GDP was likely to increase to anywhere between 9 per cent and, more probably, over 14 per cent of the world total. It seemed quite clear to me then that, under any of the four scenarios, they should play a bigger role in global decision making. In fact, it seemed so obvious that I wondered why no one else had thought of it.

Many people have quizzed me about the thinking behind the BRIC thesis, and on a basic level I often find it amusing that it is considered so profound. Four big populations becoming more productive and engaging with the rest of us in a way they hadn't previously. If they carried on doing the same, they were going to be big, plain and simple.

My colleagues Dominic Wilson and Roopa Purushothaman had helped to push the BRIC concept firmly into the mainstream with their 2003 follow-up paper, 'Dreaming with BRICs: The Path to 2050'. What they did so effectively was to compare the BRICs in 2050 to the then current world economic superpowers. 'If things go right,' they wrote, 'in less than forty years, the BRIC economies together could be larger than the G6 in dollar terms. By 2025 they could account for over half the size of the G6. Of the current G6, only the US and Japan may be among the six largest economies in US dollar terms in 2050.' Their vision of a transformed world economic order seized people's attention.

A simple chart they produced showing what they expected to be the largest economies in the world by 2050 – with China first, followed by the US, India, Japan, Brazil, Russia, UK, Germany, France and then Italy – was downloaded from the Goldman Sachs website ten times more often than any other document. It started to appear in corporate planning presentations everywhere. It propelled the reputations of both its authors, giving a huge boost to Dominic's reputation and making Roopa a superstar in India, and was the beginning of my transformation from being a forex guy to being at the centre of frequent fascinating discussions about the world economy and its development.

'Dreaming with BRICs' broke GDP growth down into three components: growth in employment, which depends largely on growth in the working-age population; growth in the capital stock, or the accumulated capital available for investment; and technical progress, a measure of productivity. Translated into nominal US-dollar GDP, a final major determinant of GDP growth is an appreciating currency in real (inflation-adjusted) terms. The research here made use of a foreign exchange model I had developed in 1995, the Goldman Sachs Dynamic Equilibrium Exchange Rate (GSDEER), to explain how currencies move. The model assumes at its basic level that the strength of a currency will reflect its relative purchasing power and relative productivity. I found that GSDEER explained much of the yen's appreciation through the 1980s and 1990s. It would probably contribute to the future of the BRICs too, if they were productive. Today a middle-income worker in India still cannot afford what a middle-income worker in America can. As India develops, though, these differences should erode, and Indians will be able to use their rupees to buy a similar amount of goods and services to their US counterparts.

To forecast as far ahead as 2050, we did not simply take the past and extrapolate into the future. Instead, we tried to create a dynamic model to reflect the changes countries go through as they develop. For population, we used the long-term projections from the United Nations to estimate the age and size of the working population. This in turn allowed us to predict the number of people whose income would enable them to pay for goods and services, to buy houses and to support those less fortunate, less able, or too young or too old to work. The model suggests that each of the BRICs will follow a different pattern. Russia's demographics often seem as bleak as Japan's or Italy's, with an ageing population and a low fertility rate. China's seem currently comparable to those of other developed European countries. In contrast, those of Brazil and especially India seem very encouraging, and by the end of 2050 their working populations should make it considerably easier for them to grow at faster rates than either China or Russia.

Some observers often latch onto the cheerless demographic profiles of China and Russia, add to this evidence their rigid political systems, and easily conclude that neither has a promising economic future. As I will discuss in more detail in the next chapter, these arguments miss some important and quite basic factors. Both China and Russia have undergone immense political changes in the past thirty years and their movement away from rigid communist systems has released their labour forces to share in the challenges and benefits of the globalized world. Moreover, in the case of China, one must consider not just its population, but the changes in the way they live, notably a marked migration to the cities. Urbanization on the scale we are seeing in China is unprecedented and providing a stimulus to growth at least comparable to that of the industrial revolution in the United Kingdom.

The BRIC growth projections for each country vary because the four do not have comparable demographics. The profile and size of their working populations will change over time and with it their growth rate. It was by blending these projections with our assumptions on the speed of productivity convergence for each of the BRICs that we ended up with decade-by-decade growth profiles for each of them. None of the BRIC countries needs to sustain growth at the level of the past decade for them soon to become collectively bigger than the G7. Even with relatively modest GDP growth rates assumed for each, they will be collectively bigger than the US before the end of 2020. From 2000 to 2010 China grew at an annual rate of more than 10 per cent. That is unlikely to repeat in the coming years, but it needs to grow at 'only' 7–8 per cent per annum for its GDP to match that of the United States by 2027.

Those countries with older populations and consequent

low fertility rates tend to be those with the slowest real GDP growth. The demographics of Japan and many of the larger continental European countries will exhibit more and more of those tendencies. In the next few decades to 2050, ageing populations in much of the G7 will pose tremendous social challenges requiring considerable changes: less generous state pension fund provision, longer working hours and an increase in retirement age. The global credit crisis of 2008 and its aftermath have accentuated the need for these changes, as the fiscal positions of these developed nations have become so weak. The International Monetary Fund has published some excellent work on these problems, especially for many of the developed G20 countries. Seen against the costs of ageing and health care, the amount governments spent on trying to halt the economic slump after the crisis appears quite manageable. These kinds of problems will doubtless affect the BRICs eventually, but not in the near future, which offers yet another reason to believe in their capacity to grow.

There are, of course, significant differences between the BRICs. In Brazil, China and India, we projected that a growing labour force would be a more important contributor to growth than in Russia, whose labour force is assumed to decline.

One graphic from the 2003 paper, reproduced here, depicted GDP growth as a race, indicating when the BRICs would be poised to win. The chart uses racing cars to illustrate when the GDP of the four BRICs, individually and collectively, would overtake the members of the G6.

China, we predicted, would soon overtake Germany, then Japan and eventually the United States by 2039. India might be the world's third largest economy within thirty years. By 2050, only the United States and Japan, of the current G6,

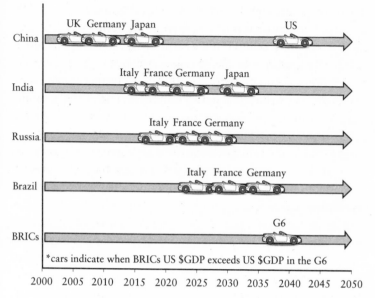

Overtaking the G6: When BRICs' US-dollar GDP Would Exceed that of the G6

Source: Dominic Wilson and Roopa Purushothaman, 'Dreaming with BRICs: The Path to 2050', Goldman Sachs Global Economics Paper No. 99, October 2003

would still be among the world's six largest economies. The other four would be the BRICs. As soon as 2040, we wrote, the combined GDP of the BRICs would exceed that of the current G6, a prospect which made nonsense of the existing world economic and social order.

Given how the BRICs have surpassed the expectations of the race-car chart above, perhaps we used the wrong cars – or didn't fill them with enough petrol.

Of course, some of this could have been said many times in the past, so we decided to look back. If anyone had undertaken a similar exercise at various points in history, then presumably they might then have reached similar conclusions to the ones we were making. How would the future have looked in 1960? We applied our methodology to eleven developed and developing countries (the US, UK, Germany, France, Italy, Japan, Brazil, Argentina, India, Korea and Hong Kong), starting in 1960 and projecting their GDP growth for the next forty years as the available data allowed. We were encouraged by what we found. In general, the growth rates projected by our model turned out to be surprisingly close to what actually happened. The model was very accurate with the developed countries, it overestimated growth in countries where government policy impeded development, such as India, Brazil and Argentina, and underestimated growth in Korea, Hong Kong and Japan. Those which had become both bigger and successful economies had combined improving demographics with rapid improvements in productivity. Those that hadn't been so successful had the benefits of the larger population but struggled to improve productivity.

The exercise helped broaden the base of our analysis even further by forcing us to consider the conditions for growth. Why had some countries managed to improve productivity when others hadn't? For the BRICs to follow the growth paths we had laid out, we felt they needed some key ingredients: a stable macroeconomic background, supported by sound macroeconomic policies that were designed to keep inflation low and public finances in good order; strong and stable political institutions; openness to trade and foreign direct investment; adaptation of modern technologies; and finally high levels of education.

The main sensitivities in our model were the rate at which the BRICs would catch up to the developed world's productivity levels; the investment rates in each country; and the demographics. We acknowledged that forecasting so far into the future carried all kinds of risks, and that any amount of bad policy or bad luck might make our forecasts redundant. But we decided that, on balance, our projections led to some important conclusions. We foresaw a radical rebalancing of the world economy, with growth in the BRICs offsetting the greying and slowing down of today's advanced economies. We could see the patterns of world investment changing, with a huge demand for investment capital in the BRICs and the evolution of large savings pools in these countries, with dramatic implications for capital markets everywhere. Rising incomes, we believed, would accelerate growth in all kinds of industries as consumption patterns changed, which in turn would transform the demand for commodities. Global companies could benefit enormously from the growth of the BRIC consumer, but would be faced with fresh strategic choices between investing in countries which had the largest GDPs per se and those with the largest GDPs per capita, a question of the biggest versus the richest. And there were the regional consequences, with the BRICs' neighbours looking set to profit from their ascent, and accumulation of geopolitical influence.

The dramatic changes we were predicting were perhaps best summarized by the question with which readers were challenged at the end of the report: 'Are you ready?'

GROWTH ENVIRONMENT SCORES

By 2005, when Dominic, Roopa, and I together with another colleague, Anna Stupnytska, wrote our next major review of the BRICs, we had evolved our understanding and measurement of their growth prospects even further by introducing a measure called the growth environment score (GES). We drew primarily on the World Bank's World Development Indicators Database to develop scores out of ten for thirteen categories. No ranking system like this can ever be perfect, but we felt it gave us a reasonable means of forecasting a country's chances of converging on the developed world's income levels. We thought it might keep us truly objective about the path to the future.

Economists believe that higher productivity is critical for sustaining growth and helping to improve welfare. What is not known is exactly what causes productivity to increase. If it were so easy, then growth would be more predictable, achievable and easy to attain. Many countries, developed and developing, might have risen to be on an economic par with the United States.

The GES Index

Macroeconomic variables

Inflation
Government deficit
Investment spending
External debt
Degree of openness

Microeconomic variables

Use of mobile telephones
Use of the internet
Use of computers
Life expectancy
Education
Rule of law
Corruption
Stability of government

The GES index consists of thirteen different variables, five macroeconomic in nature, and eight microeconomic (see table). We simply average out the scores without giving one variable any more weight than another. To be more accurate, we should probably apply economic tests to each variable to assess its impact on productivity, and from this derive a weighting system. (Whether this would make a big difference to the scores is open to debate.)

Education is perhaps the most important variable in driving the working population to higher productivity. In our scoring system, we originally used a simple measure, average number of years young people spend in secondary education. From 2007 we began using the more accurate measure of net secondary school enrolment, i.e. the share of children of official school age that are enrolled in secondary school. We settled on our standard for its simplicity, comparability and reliability. It was measurable across many countries and seemed a reasonable predictor of economic success. Of the BRICs, Brazil, China and Russia appear to be more successful than India in terms of provision of the most basic education.

Linked to educational attainment is the use of technology, which also leads to faster productivity gains. In our GES index, we measure the use of telephones or mobiles, personal computers and the internet separately. All are important, but for developing countries mobile phone use may be the most significant. The World Bank has estimated that for every 10 per cent increase in mobile phone penetration, GDP per capita rises by 0.7 per cent in developing countries. Mobile banking, for example, allows countries to skip entire phases of development, such as the building of a retail banking system, with multiple high-street branches.

Government is another obvious factor in a country's ability to become more productive, because it is the government that provides the appropriate framework and support system for growth as well as incentives. Nations whose leaders constantly struggle to cope with change or with the implementation of new and different ideas are typically those that have poor productivity performances and low growth rates. Stability, credibility, the rule of law and the absence of corruption are also key to allowing economies to grow.

Equally important are macroeconomic factors. A low and stable level of inflation is critical for productivity as businesses are loath to take risks and plan when the future is uncertain. Economies in which governments restrict overall spending to affordable levels and maintain a modest debt also appear to be economies that can maintain higher productivity performances. The degree to which countries participate in international trade is likely to be another important influence on growth.

Classical international development theory suggests that as countries develop, they raise their productivity performance towards the levels of more developed countries. Helped by international capital flows, especially foreign direct investment, countries are willing to change and adopt or copy best practices and introduce the higher standards of the more developed nations. In this manner, their ability to become more productive increases. Of course, countries see their productivity potential adapt at different speeds, depending on many factors. The GES, calculated on an index from 1 to 10, was our attempt to capture them. The higher the score, the more productive the country. Trying to forecast without taking these social measures into account would have been an exercise in purely theoretical economics.

In 2005, China's GES ranked highest among the BRICs, followed by Russia, Brazil and India. China performed best on macroeconomic stability, openness to trade and education, but was less strong on corruption and technology. Brazil was less good on education and its government deficit, but better in terms of political stability and life expectancy. Russia's main weaknesses were political stability, corruption and inflation, while India did well on rule of law but poorly in terms of education, technology adoption, its fiscal position and openness. By 2010 Brazil ranked the highest with GES of 5.5, China second (5.4), somewhat ahead of Russia (4.8), with India on 4.0 a distant fourth. As I will discuss in the next chapter, all the BRICs need to improve their growth environment scores or they will fail to reach their potential. A good benchmark would be South Korea, whose GES in 2010 stood at 7.6, a level higher than all the G7 countries except Canada. I'm sure if in ten or twenty years from now, each of the BRIC countries has such a relatively high GES, their economies will be both much bigger and wealthier.

As a measurement tool the growth environment scores have proved extremely useful. We now calculate them for 180 countries, and they have played a significant role in our thinking about the N-11 growth economies as we defined them in 2005, and which I will explore later.

Having explained how we reached our various projections for the BRICs, I should say that my only regret is that we weren't bolder.

Between 2001 and 2010, the BRIC economies' GDP rose much more sharply than I had thought possible even in the most optimistic scenario. Moreover, their citizens' wealth showed equally remarkable increases, bringing hundreds of millions of people out of poverty. Their GDP per capita, the best indication of individual wealth, collectively trebled.

China started the decade as the biggest of the BRICs and

has remained so. Brazil was the second big surprise for us, at least in monetary terms. Including it among the BRICs was my biggest gamble, but by 2010 it had overtaken Italy to become the seventh largest economy in the world, with a GDP of $2.1 trillion. I never imagined Brazil could grow so big so fast. Our racing-car graphic didn't suggest it would reach that stage until after 2020. India and Russia also surpassed my forecasts for both nominal and real GDP growth.

Some commentators claim that these observations overstate the impact of BRIC growth, that it was the product of a freakish and unrepeatable set of circumstances: rapid export

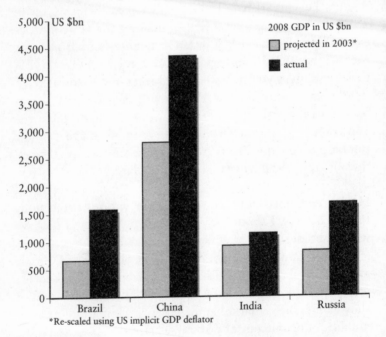

All Four BRICs Have Grown Larger than Predicted
Source: Goldman Sachs Global ECS Research

growth, the commodity boom and unsustainable US demand. Yet if the numbers are viewed from a demand perspective, rather than GDP, and omitting exports, then an even stronger picture of BRIC growth emerges. While there is no doubting China's remarkable export progress in the last decade, this is not the whole story. More significant is the rise of the Chinese consumer. Even the conservative official Chinese data indicate that personal consumption rose by $1.5 trillion between 2001 and 2011, the equivalent of creating another United Kingdom. China is no longer just a low-cost labour phenomenon. Its people are rapidly rising up the income ladder and spending.

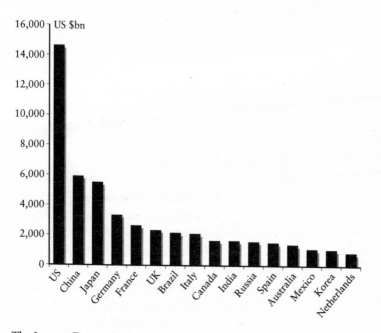

The Largest Economies in 2010

Source: International Monetary Fund, *World Economic Outlook 2010*

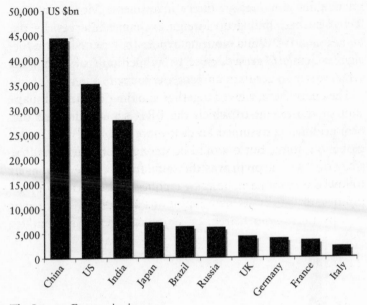

The Largest Economies in 2050

Source: Dominic Wilson and Roopa Purushothaman, 'Dreaming with BRICs: The Path to 2050', Goldman Sachs Global Economics Paper No. 99, October 2003

The BRICs' role in world trade is also expanding faster than we first thought and certainly much faster than world trade overall. Trade within the BRICs has accelerated sharply, largely because Brazil and Russia supply so many of the commodities needed by China and India. This pattern looks set to continue in the next decade and beyond, forcing adjustments to these countries' foreign exchange policies. BRIC leaders are already discussing alternatives to using the US dollar as their main trading currency.

The BRICs, notably China and Brazil, have become powerful magnets for foreign direct investment. Moreover, they have also been piling up foreign exchange reserves. By the middle of 2011 China alone held more than $3 trillion in foreign exchange reserves, close to 50 per cent of their own GDP, vastly larger than any other country in the world.

The charts here, viewed together, should give a useful snapshot of the extent to which the BRICs outperformed our projections and assumed an ever more powerful role in the global economy. But it would be wrong to conclude that the story of BRIC growth was the same for each country. Each followed its own path, beset by unique challenges and opportunities, driven by its own ambitions and attacked at every step by those who feared, or simply could not fathom, its rise.

3

BRIC by BRIC

Ever since I first wrote about the BRICs, people have suggested I modify the acronym – some jokingly, many seriously. I have been told it should be CRIBs, as these were economies in their economic infancy. Or that I should drop one of the letters. Did the R deserve to be in there? Or the B? India and China were obvious inclusions, though over the years and through several serious economic wobbles, there were times when I wondered if the vision I laid out for them would ever come true. I've occasionally thought that I'm going to be woken from sleep one morning by the US Securities and Exchange Commission threatening me because I predicted China would be the biggest economy in the world. But that's the reality of making a big, long-term forecast like this. There are bound to be bumps along the way.

Our models were designed to accommodate different rates of growth, as the BRICs reached different stages of development. GDP is, after all, a headline number which can conceal many aspects of growth, especially its quality. Many people looking at China in 2011, for example, compare it to Japan in the early 1990s, and there are headline similarities. Back then, many people were saying it was only a matter of time before Japan overtook America to become the largest economy in the world. Instead, Japan's investment bubble popped. Property values plummeted. A low birth rate coupled with a refusal to admit immigrants meant Japan's population stagnated. There was no one to fuel fresh growth.

Today, we see some fast-rising asset values in China and hear talk of it soon overtaking the US as the world's largest economy. The difference with Japan in the 1990s is that China still has lots of room to grow. Hundreds of millions of people have yet to become part of the economic transformation in the country, urbanization is probably only half complete, and all these people are yet to become wealthy consumers. The correct comparison for China would be the Japan of the 1960s or 1970s, when there were still huge opportunities for productivity improvement. The headlines may lead some analysts to compare the Japan of 1990 and the China of 2011, but dig deeper and you find significant differences.

China and the other BRICs have a long way to go before they need to settle for the mature, Western, steady-state growth rate of around 2.5 per cent. Our model for BRIC growth to 2050 averages Chinese growth at 5.5 per cent over the period, though it falls to 3.5 per cent in the final decade. We know that as countries develop and their populations stabilize, their growth rate naturally slows. This will occur in the BRICs, as it does everywhere, but not for many years to come.

The collective growth numbers, of course, are only one piece of the puzzle. To understand fully what the BRICs are all about, it is necessary to examine each country individually, and that is what I shall be doing in this chapter.

BRAZIL

The first time I went to Brazil was in 2003 to give a speech about the BRIC dream. Just as I was about to speak, the man who had invited me whispered in my ear, 'The only reason you included Brazil was so you had a nice-sounding acronym.' Even Brazilians could not believe that the long-impossible economic dream had a chance of becoming reality.

Because expectations were so low, the moment I got home from that trip, I decided to buy some Brazilian reals. After about three months, I sold them, but that was a mistake, because over the past six years, it has been a spectacularly strong currency. If I had told any of those foreign currency traders I hung out with in the 1980s that one of the strongest currencies this decade would be the Brazilian real, they would have laughed at me. But, of course, that is what has happened.

Brazil today is the most popular of the BRICs so far as foreign direct investment is concerned and I am constantly invited to speak at forums in São Paulo and Rio. Investors, ranging from global private equity firms to hedge funds, are battling it out to acquire Brazilian assets. I would frequently visit Tokyo and meet representatives of various Japanese retail banks, who told me that conservative Japanese house-wives, the mythical Mrs Watanabes, were very excited to invest in the real. This has now been the case for years. Some time ago, I met the head of a South African bank who told me he was considering investing in a Brazilian bank. The whole world now sees that Brazil's economic transformation, from hyperinflationary basket case to a potential twenty-first-century Latin American superpower, finally had legs.

Just as China proved its maturity during the 1997 Asian

financial crisis, Brazil showed its mettle in the 2008 global one. In the past, Brazil would have been guaranteed to be at the heart of the storm, its currency, interest and inflation rates careening all over the place. But they did not succumb to the crisis. Instead, they cut rates on the back of it, managed their way through it and recovered quickly and easily. Stable policies over the previous decade allowed the country's leaders to implement expansionary policies at a time when other countries were being backed into a corner. This was virtually unheard of for a major developing economy, and certainly for Brazil. The boom we saw in Brazil in 2008–9, while so much of the world suffered, surprised many, adding to the intensity of the markets' rising love affair with the country.

Popularity, though, has its price. These days I do worry that Brazil might be partially suffering from the so-called 'Dutch disease'. As a result of the country's richness in commodity wealth, and with its high interest rates, the currency might have risen too far too fast, and this may damage the manufacturing part of the economy. So many Brazilian investors who visit my office in London tell me they find London cheap. Such a rarely heard observation is a reflection of the real's strength. In mid-2011, Brazil possibly has the most overvalued currency of the BRICs. In the long term, I remain extremely optimistic about Brazil, and its recent successes, after decades of economic failure, are grounds for great hope. In the shorter term, I suspect that the strength of the real will be problematical.

As I've said, the decision to include Brazil among the BRICs was far from automatic. I wasn't necessarily looking for a Latin American companion for the other three but Brazil, with its population exceeding 180 million and its policymakers finally prepared to target inflation, stood out. But many were sceptical and some, including some Brazilians, even begged me not to include it. Our 2003 paper laying out the path to 2050 for the BRICs included a large, separate section on Brazil setting out conditions and reasons to consider Brazil separately from Russia, India and China.

Goldman's own Brazilian economist, Paulo Leme, shared the concerns of many. Paulo had very good historical reasons to be worried for his country. Brazil, after all, had always been 'the country of the future' which somehow never got there. Its vast territory and abundant natural resources reeked of economic potential. For much of the twentieth century it was one of the fastest-growing countries in the world, and attracted millions of immigrants. In the 1950s foreign investment began to pour in and multinationals set up offices in the country. In the 1960s people predicted that Brazil and Argentina would soon be the biggest economies in the world. Inflation and inept, highly centralized political leadership killed that dream. Brazil was undone by perpetual economic and political crises, alternating between democracy and military dictatorship; periods of vibrant economic growth were followed by extreme slumps. Governments would point to the high levels of foreign investment and the success of Brazil's football team and talk of their country in superlatives. Brazil had the world's longest bridge and the world's largest hydroelectric plant. But these boasts could not conceal the fact that the country rarely achieved the stability essential for making serious economic progress. Its growth was uneven and unequally shared. Living conditions for the country's rural and urban poor were a stain on its reputation. Its cities became notorious for their violence. A dismal low was reached in São Paulo in 1997 when 8,092 people were murdered, an average of nearly one murder per hour. In my professional lifetime, Brazil has had six different currencies, a reflection of the economic chaos which has plagued the country. The problems of corruption and inefficiency were endemic. And for ordinary people, that manifested itself in runaway inflation that made shopping a nightmare and saving impossible.

Since 1950 the country had grown at an annual rate averaging 5.3 per cent, but between 1995 and 2005 that slowed to 2.9 per cent. This was a consequence of a painful economic readjustment which transformed Brazil's economic destiny. In the 1990s alone, Brazil went through three financial crises. But a group of key politicians and economists, notably Fernando Henrique Cardoso, the president who first took office in the mid-1990s, identified hyperinflation as Brazil's curse and decided to fight it. After decades of relying on external financing, Brazil finally engaged in the hard work of stabilizing its currency. Its government's harsh cost-cutting lowered investment in infrastructure and reduced the country's capital stock. Inflation was finally brought under control. But the benefits of this macro stabilization plan took time to feed through into higher growth. We argued in 2003 that Brazil still had important reforms to make, such as opening itself up to trade, cutting its debt-to-GDP ratio and allowing the private sector into the debt markets, and raising its investment and savings rate. Without these, we feared, Brazil might continue to underperform the other BRICs. As we wrote in 2003, our hopes for Brazil 'may still prove too optimistic without deeper structural reforms'.

Everything else about Brazil was immensely appealing: its culture, its sport and its resources. It has always been an easy country to love. Once its economy turned, the world was ready to embrace it. Brazil's rise as an economic power has happened far more quickly, at least in US-dollar terms, than we envisaged back in 2001 and 2003. While this is largely due to the remarkable rise of the real against the dollar and many other currencies, it is also recognition of the more stable and improved growth rate. By the end of 2010, Brazil's economy had reached $2.1 trillion. This has happened much sooner than we expected. In our 2050 projections, we assumed some real appreciation of the BRIC currencies, but not to this degree. There is the danger that the real in 2011 is overvalued, which brings its own risks, notably increasing the cost of all-important exports – and the risk at any moment of a large and messy reversal in the real. Its upward trend may need to be reversed in the coming years for Brazil's growth to be more sustainable.

But turning back again to the macro framework, the basic economic facts about Brazil are stunning. It has the fifth largest population in the world, and it's one that is young and growing. As the growth of the United States has demonstrated, having a rising young population can lead to very strong and prosperous economic growth. And as the 2050 projections show, Brazil has the potential to be much bigger. It has the capacity to become an economy close to $10 trillion, about five times bigger than it is today. On a relative basis, Brazil has the potential to overtake Germany and Japan – although it is unlikely that it could ever reach the size of the US or, of course, China. While it is the second largest BRIC today, it is likely that India will overtake Brazil at some stage in the next ten years or so, just because of the sheer number of Indians. But if Brazil can continue down the path of the past ten to fifteen years, then its population has a good chance of delivering genuine GDP growth and allowing the country to match its economic potential.

An important change in Brazil has been the transformation in its political culture. Many people worried that when Luiz Inácio Lula da Silva, the head of the Workers' Party, became president in 2003, he might reverse the economic policies of his predecessors. He was feared by many to be a left-wing fanatic who would undo President Cardoso's economic policies in favour of populist measures that would excite his supporters. I might have shared their worries, but Lula did two things that reassured me. He both promised his support for a policy of inflation targeting, and then he delivered it in the form of a new Growth Acceleration Programme although no longer through Arminio Fraga, the early driver of the policy, who had been replaced by Henrique Meirelles as head of the Brazilian central bank. That was enough for me. In retrospect, he looks like the greatest G20 policymaker of the first decade of the twenty-first century. He succeeded in persuading the lower classes in Brazil that Western policies are good for them. Whatever pain inflation targeting might bring in terms of monetary discipline, it was certainly better than never knowing the value of the money in your pocket. Lula had grown up poor and knew how devastating hyperinflation and constant financial insecurity could be. He made a convincing advocate of the policies necessary for a developing economy to grow.

In September 2010, the *Financial Times*' weekly 'Lunch with the FT' feature was an interview with Fernando Henrique Cardoso at a restaurant in São Paulo.[1] I was asked to write a short piece to accompany the interview, which gave me a chance to compare his legacy with that of Lula's. I started by saying that few things would give me more pleasure than to have my own *FT* lunch, sipping caipirinhas on the beach at Ipanema and listening to a debate between Cardoso and Lula. Though very different men, Lula is in many ways Cardoso's heir. Cardoso gave him the platform to succeed and Lula was smart enough to keep most of what he inherited while translating the benefits of stability to the many, enabling people to rise up the income scale. This in turn gave policymakers the credibility needed to persist with stability-orientated policy. As Cardoso put it in his interview, 'I did the reforms, Lula surfed the wave.'

In 2010 the political mantle passed to Lula's successor Dilma Rousseff. The challenge for her lies in improving Brazil's growth environment scores to ensure the country can continue to grow. In 2011, Brazil's scores were the highest among the BRICs, but there is a danger that the country's economic success may have, to use Cardoso's word, 'anaesthetized' Brazil to the need to keep the reforming momentum. Brazil is now home to giant companies such as Petrobras, which in September 2010 launched the world's largest share offering, of $67 billion, to fund exploitation of some of the world's largest oil reserves. Yet in 2010 Brazil ranked just 127th out of 183 countries in the World Bank's yearly 'Doing Business' survey. The country still needs reforms in areas ranging from taxation to infrastructure. Brazilian democracy will require large-scale new programmes to improve the quality of health care and education, and increase the use of technology. For all its successes, Brazil's growth environment score is still two points lower than that of South Korea, perhaps a sign of how far it has to go before it can be considered a fully developed economy.

At some point, the country will have to reverse the spending unleashed to counter the effects of the financial crisis, increase its role in international trade and expand private sector investment. Despite an encouraging rise in foreign direct investment, Brazil remains more closed to world trade than it should. The government ought to be encouraging its companies to explore more international opportunities. Boosting private sector investment will be difficult, given that interest rates are still extremely high, despite the long and successful battle to stabilize inflation. Whether this is because Brazilian citizens doubt the longevity of low inflation or it is a symptom of 'crowding out' by government spending is debatable, but both are possibly true. Reversing the post-crisis increase in government spending might help lower interest rates and ease some of the upward pressure on the real.

As I've already said, the strength of the Brazilian currency is another challenge. I suspect that the relatively high level of interest rates is helping sustain it, especially given the lack of yield available in most other major markets. If Mrs Watanabe is buying the real for its yields, then you can assume a lot of other people are. But there may be other reasons for the real's strength. It may reflect the desire of business people all over the world to invest in the country when they'd ignored it in the past. The only way of knowing for sure would be if Brazilian interest rates fell. It could be that Brazil's interest rates are where they ought to be, and that it's the rates in other countries which are too low. According to this argument, rates around the globe will eventually rise, narrowing the differential between Brazil's levels and the rest of the world's. In any case, high interest rates have not stopped Brazil from growing strongly in recent years and so cannot be seen as an insuperable obstacle.

But the most important thing Ms Rousseff can do, in my judgement, is to make sure that the central bank stays independent and is allowed to pursue its own path for keeping inflation low and stable. Brazil's life as a BRIC has created the potential for its economic rebirth. Low and stable inflation gives every Brazilian the chance to plan more sensibly for the future, an underestimated plank of sustainable growth. As I write in mid-2011, Brazil's average wealth is around $10,000 per head, a dramatic rise in the past decade. Tens of millions of Brazilians have risen out of poverty. By 2050 Brazil's wealth may approach levels currently enjoyed by the best of the developed countries, at least four times those of today. This would not only make Brazil one of the wealthiest of the increasingly inappropriately so-called 'developing economies', but at last a country of today and not just of the future.

In 2010 the Mayor of Rio de Janeiro, Eduardo Paes, visited me in my office in London. Rio will be holding the Olympics in 2016, four years after London in 2012, and the mayor wanted to learn from London's preparations. He invited me to come and talk at a BRIC conference in Rio. The proposed date wasn't going to work, but he is a charismatic man and he persisted. He said, 'How about we organize it the week of the Rio Carnival?' As it turned out, that coincided with a holiday period for me and my wife.

Although I was in Rio primarily for business, we made sure that I had time for a personal holiday. Naturally, part of it involved my second ever visit to watch a game at the Maracanã, the city's great football stadium. I also had the opportunity to visit Rio's largest favela, one of the urban areas most people think of as desperate slums. I had visited Rio for the first time in 2003, and had read endless stories of the city's crime and poverty, of violent thefts along the streets around Copacabana. I had always been intrigued by the favelas, so visiting Rio's biggest was an exciting experience. We were surprised by how organized and reasonably normal it seemed. Compared with slum areas of cities in India, it didn't seem too bad to us.

It was a blazing hot day, and at one point we stopped for a drink in a tiny bar. As I was sitting there, I noticed a travel agency next door. In its windows were advertisements for flights around Brazil and the world. When I asked some of the locals about this, they said that the presence of a travel agency within a favela was just another sign of their country's progress. Of course, this was just one favela, we visited during the daytime, and Rio is not necessarily representative of Brazil. But overall this trip significantly influenced my perceptions of the country, adding texture to the raw economic data.

I left full of admiration for the diversity and tolerance of the Brazilian people. I had never properly appreciated what a melting pot Brazil is, with so many people of different colours, and ethnic and national origins, living happily alongside each other on the beaches of Copacabana and Ipanema and throughout the city.

Eduardo Paes and his team have a plan to make Rio the City of the Southern Hemisphere, a competitor to Sydney and Cape Town, as well as to Latin American rivals such as Buenos Aires. It's a challenge. But given the city's natural beauty, provided they can improve its infrastructure, notably its airport, expand its facilities and reduce crime, it's a fantastic goal that is perhaps achievable. It will certainly be helped by the 2014 World Cup in Brazil and the 2016 Summer Olympics in Rio. These will be huge opportunities to highlight Brazil's strengths and spur the country to ever more improvement. The Chinese certainly viewed the 2008 Beijing

Olympics that way. At the very least, the sporting events should improve Rio's hotel situation. Along the sixteen kilometres of Copacabana and Ipanema beachfront, there are still just two five-star hotels. Contrast that with Miami, where luxury hotels line almost the entire oceanfront.

When my host whispered to me in 2003 that Brazil was only included among the BRICs to make the acronym sound better, it made me realize how low expectations were for the country. It didn't have to improve that much to surprise people. In fact, over the past few years, Brazil has surprised people a lot and while there remain many challenges, Brazil might also have lots of exciting potential ahead.

RUSSIA

It is hard to find people quite so optimistic about Russia. In fact it is the one country many think should be dropped from the BRICs. It is not a view I share. But the argument goes that Russia's unfavourable demographics, excessive dependence on energy and raw materials and its poor record in governance and legal structures make it an unworthy recipient of the power bestowed by its status as a BRIC. I frequently receive emails explaining to me why BRIC should in fact be BIC.

What I tell these critics is that, while Russia does have serious challenges, it also has the potential to have a higher GDP per capita than the other BRICs, and even higher than all other European countries. If Russia fulfils its potential, it will create all sorts of interesting and complex political and social issues for the European Union and the world, besides the obvious economic ones. For the EU to have a wealthier neighbour on its borders would be quite remarkable. Provided it does not provoke conflict, it could raise the possibility of Russian membership of the EU.

At the core of Russia's present challenges are its demographics. It is widely believed that Russia has a troubling economic future as its population may decline sharply owing to excessively high mortality. This widespread expectation is at the core of why so many doubt Russia's worth to be regarded in the same context as China, India and even Brazil. Anecdotes about Russia's poor life expectancy abound. I was once told a story by a Russian academic that 60 per cent of all Russian males over the age of forty die drunk. True or not, it feeds a certain prejudice about Russian life. During my many discussions about Russia over the years, one of the statistics which hooked people's attention was that the average Russian male lived to only fifty-nine. That's twenty years less than the average American man. At a BRIC conference in London in May 2010, I had the pleasure of interviewing First Deputy Prime Minister Igor Shuvalov, who told me that male life expectancy had risen closer to sixty-five as a result of major policy initiatives to reduce the consumption of very low-quality alcohol, especially vodka. When I discussed these comments with academics, they questioned the degree of improvement, but agreed that life expectancy was on the rise. Smarter taxation to discourage consumption of low-quality vodka was cited by them as a critical variable.

Improving Russia's demographics has certainly been on the minds of its leaders. In 2006 Vladimir Putin, then president, now prime minister, called demography 'Russia's most acute problem today' and the situation 'critical'.[2] Its population had been falling since the collapse of the Soviet Union owing to a combination of emigration, rising death rates and falling birth rates. HIV had also taken its toll. In 2004, just 10.4 babies were born for every 16 Russians who died. All across Russia, it was rare to see a family with more than one child. Economists and sociologists argued over the causes. Some blamed the sudden disappearance of the Soviet welfare system and its replacement by a more anarchic free market. One scholar wrote that 'the Russian crisis is not due to a single disease, or even a small set of microbial horrors, [rather] a constellation of occurrences that include not only infectious disease, but alcoholism, drug abuse, suicide, trauma injuries, astounding levels of cardiovascular disease, male/female estrangement and loss of family cohesion, declining physiological fertility, ugly environmental pollution and micronutrient starvation'.[3] Whatever the causes, if Russia had failed to act, its population might have fallen to below 100 million by 2050. Putin proposed a wide range of subsidies and financial incentives to increase Russia's birth rate, including raising child benefit (payable for eighteen months) to $53 a month for a first child and about $107 for a second child, longer periods of maternity leave, and investment in prenatal care, maternity hospitals and kindergartens. Parents who had a second child were promised $10,000 from the government. The goal was to reverse Russia's annual population decline of 700,000 per year.

By 2007, the government was claiming progress.[4] The health minister reported that the number of two-child families had risen by 8 per cent in a year. Some Russian methods for promoting fertility could seem amusing to outsiders. A monument to motherhood was erected near Moscow. In 2007 the city of Ulyanovsk organized a day of conception, when workers were encouraged to go home and have sex. Prizes including a 4x4 car were given to those who gave birth on 12 June, Russia Day, the following year.

In April 2011 Prime Minister Putin returned to the issue, promising to spend over $50 billion to increase Russia's birth rate by up to 30 per cent by 2015. Preliminary results from a national survey in 2010 showed that Russia's population had fallen by 2.2 million since 2002, to just under 143 million. When I highlighted this speech to a number of my colleagues at Goldman Sachs Asset Management it was, as Russian policies usually are, met with scepticism by most. Interestingly the sceptics did not include Clemens Grafe, the GS Russian economist. He suggested that boosting the birth rate by 25 per cent by 2015 would be easily attainable as it was already 20 per cent above 2006 levels.

If Russia can pull off this demographic shift its economic prospects will improve dramatically. Our forecasts for 2050 will suddenly look far too pessimistic, and the 'lazy consensus' will be in for a shock.

Based only on our conservative consensus demographic assumptions, Russia's GDP could grow to $7 trillion by 2050, around four times where it is today. If its population simply stops declining Russia could quite easily become as large as Brazil at around $10 trillion in 2050. To reach the potential we outlined in 2003, Russia needs 'only' to grow annually by around 3 per cent. This is important to bear in mind in view of the 'gloom' about Russia's potential. Russia doesn't need dramatic growth rates. It just needs to avoid crises. If it were to achieve this, its GDP could overtake that of Italy as soon as 2017, and in the decade 2020 to 2030, steadily sweep past France, the UK and ultimately Germany. It is quite something to imagine that within twenty-five years from 2011, Russia could have an economy larger than Germany's.

Nonetheless, I notice a high degree of antipathy towards Russia – and it is understandable how casual observation can lead to this sort of view. In fact, particularly in the case of both Russia and China, spending so much time on the BRICs encourages me to think about what kind of government is best suited both for economic growth and for the different stages of the growth evolution. In the West, former President Gorbachev is regarded as a hero for ending communism in the Soviet Union. But in Russia he is considered weak, a failure as a leader. Meanwhile Putin is seen by many in Russia as strong and decisive. His authoritarian methods are commonly accepted there as essential to Russian strength.

A Russian friend once told me that I need to understand two things about Russian political leadership. The first was that there were a lot of tools from the Soviet state which were still lying around, and the temptation to pick them up and use them was great. Russians over forty will remember well all aspects of the Soviet days, including many of those who were employed to keep order. The second was that, if Russia is to progress towards a more Western model of democratic society, it needs to take three steps forward, then two steps back. Without the occasional reversal, he argues, Russia can't drag its people onward. It might be too rapid a change for them to deal with. Russia's history has been so chaotic and volatile that it simply could not be ignored if the country were to hurtle on unchecked. Russia needs to be nursed forward in a way consistent with its past, not violently shoved into an uncertain future as it was under Yeltsin. Putin's and Medvedev's approach reflects that need.

Yet Western investors often fail to take all this into account. All they see is political regression. In 1997 Russia became part of the G8. The G7 decided that Russia, under President Yeltsin, might quickly become a Western-style democracy and acquire all the trappings of a G7 nation. Its 140 million people had been recently released from decades of communism and seemed eager to realize their economic potential. By 2001, though, there was growing apprehension among Western politicians about Russia's ability or willingness to join the capitalist ranks. Yeltsin's successor Putin had put a halt to some of the more aggressive free-market policies. His authoritarian methods seemed a throwback to Tsarist rule. Such doubts have only intensified since then.

Nevertheless, Russia is still bursting with potential. Its population dwarfs that of Europe's largest country, Germany. If it can embrace the best of Western technology and become a more hospitable home for foreign investment it could still grow very quickly.

In early 2011 I attended the St Petersburg Economic Forum, a kind of Russian version of the World Economic Forum, which meets annually in Davos in the Swiss Alps. At a discussion about the internet, one of my fellow panellists pointed out that two of the Russian internet companies that had gone public in the previous twelve months were among the most highly valued technology companies in Europe, the Middle East and Africa. The UK, France and Germany cannot boast similar successes. During this same discussion, President Medvedev himself came in to participate, an indication of Russian interest at the highest level. The Skolkovo Innovation Centre being developed just outside Moscow is intended to nurture a Silicon Valley-style technology cluster and both

Apple and Cisco have invested. I believe Russia has one of the best national technology policies in the world, with the raw intellectual talent to make it happen. Russia's history of strong centrally guided education with very high standards in both maths and science enable it easily to increase both its use of modern technology and its innovative application. Not only is this apparent in business, it is also appealing to the country's policymakers.

Technology, however, is just one element of the growth environment score. On the others, Russia clearly needs to do better. Out of the 180 countries we track, Russia's GES ranks 110th. It is third among the BRICs, ahead of just India. High commodity prices over the past decade have allowed Russia to shore up its fiscal and external accounts, though the sharp fall in crude oil prices in 2008 revealed its vulnerability. With luck this crisis will persuade Russia's leaders to diversify and reduce their reliance on natural resources.

At a micro level, Russia is strong in education (better than India) and communications: telephones, computers, the internet. Its weaknesses, aside from low life expectancy, are political stability, the rule of law, corruption and the general creep of government into important aspects of everyday decision making. Russia's failings in these areas tend to kindle an emotional hostility in the West. But it is important to keep some perspective. After all, Italy arguably has had weak rule of law for a long time, but its economy has rolled along for years. I think there are some grounds for optimism in Russia. Those policymakers I meet tend to be highly intelligent, literate people who understand Russia's situation and its options. The same goes for the so-called 'oligarchs'. In any other country, these men would be known simply as businessmen, perhaps 'moguls' or 'tycoons'. The fact that when

they're Russian we call them 'oligarchs' reveals our own fanciful, romantic prejudices about the country. I've met a number
of them one-on-one and they're no different from any number
of successful European or American business people.

What strikes me on my frequent trips to Russia is that Russians don't seem to crave Western democracy in the way we
think they might. Outside Russia, Vladimir Putin is often
portrayed with disdain as an autocrat. At home he is popular,
despite a deep recession following the global credit crisis.
Foreign observers need to remember that past presidents
Yeltsin and Gorbachev were never seen as popular leaders
inside Russia, and they are still not regarded with anything
like the admiration or reverence they received in the West.
Under them, Russians did not see their wealth climb. They
led during unstable and difficult times.

Of course, I'm not blind to the challenges Russia presents.
In 2003 I visited Moscow to meet Bill Browder, an American
investor, who was hugely enthusiastic about investing in Russia. He told me what a great thing Russia was, and he was a
keen evangelist for its inclusion among the BRICs, as it
helped him raise money for his funds. Bill was an active
investor in individual stocks and often made public pro-
nouncements about how companies were being run, and how
some might be better run. Some years ago, he had his visa
revoked and would probably face tough consequences if he
tried to return there.

There is no better illustration of the debate about growing
state corporatism than the story of Yukos Oil. In the early
2000s it seemed as though Yukos might become one of the
biggest and best oil companies in the world. Today it doesn't
exist. In 2003 its former CEO, Mikhail Khodorkovsky, was

arrested and charged with fraud. Yukos was accused of avoiding enormous tax liabilities, its assets were sold off cheaply at auction and the company was declared bankrupt. Most of its top executives fled the country, but Khodorkovsky, who had once been the wealthiest man in Russia and the sixteenth richest man in the world (according to *Forbes* magazine), was tried, convicted and sent to jail. From prison he has been a thorn in the Kremlin's side, writing letters and speeches which accuse Putin and Medvedev of running a corrupt political and legal system, and warning Westerners against investing in Russia.

The arguments over Yukos continue. Many in the West believe Khodorkovsky's claims that Yukos was dismantled simply as an act of political revenge, as it had become too big and powerful for the Kremlin. Russian commentators, especially those close to the Kremlin, accuse Western observers of not recognizing the illegal behaviour of Yukos, supposedly including its systematic tax avoidance. Somewhere in the middle are those who say that even if Yukos didn't pay its taxes, its punishment was extreme and indicative of the many problems facing anyone trying to do business in Russia. The relationships between Russia's politicians and the so-called 'oligarchs' remain mysterious and worrying to outside investors. The baffling deaths of business people, politicians and journalists who oppose the Kremlin don't help either.

These things probably explain why Russian equities have underperformed compared to other BRIC markets since the financial crisis, and appear to be relatively 'cheap'. The Russian market trades at a lower valuation than other BRIC markets because the expected profit one year ahead is much harder to forecast owing to uncertainty about Russia's future. In the early years of the BRICs, Russia used to trade at a premium to Brazil but now trades at a significant discount.

Another major concern about Russia is its over-reliance on oil and natural gas. In one sense, it is a great blessing for a country to have large energy and mineral resources which it can sell. But it risks inducing laziness. It is wonderful when commodity prices are rising, but when they fall an economy can quickly look vulnerable. This happened to Russia in 2008 during the global financial crisis, when its GDP fell by 8 per cent as a result of the fall in oil prices, and the value of its stock market fell a staggering 70 per cent. No country likes to experience such volatility. If Russia is to achieve its ultimate BRIC potential of multiplying its 2010 GDP several times over by 2050, it has to move beyond energy and develop other companies in other industries, and to widen economic wealth ownership in its populace. President Medvedev's plans for reducing the importance of energy announced in 2009 linked to his goals to boost the technology industry are definitely a step in the necessary direction. A well-educated and technologically literate population should make this goal attainable.

Russia should also do more to encourage foreign consumer multinationals, especially those with strong brand names, to enter Russia. Keeping ownership of the natural resource companies is perhaps understandable, but in terms of satisfying rising consumer aspirations of Russians, allowing foreign companies access to its market would make more sense than trying to develop home-grown Russian rivals. Pepsi Cola's acquisition of Wimm-Bill-Dann, Russia's biggest food company, in late 2010 might be an important positive sign in this regard.

Russia could become very wealthy. Russian GDP per capita could rise from $10,000 today to $20,000 by 2020 and perhaps close to $60,000 by 2050. Its demand for consumer products could grow to match that of many developed countries today. In 2010 there were already believed to be more car owners in Russia than in Germany, mainly due to its larger population, but also due to the rapidly rising wealth. If Russia's political leaders could provide a supportive environment, they will probably attract the big multinational motor manufacturers.

Russia could also become a desirable location for other multinationals seeking to export to the former Soviet states as well as to Iran, Iraq and other Middle Eastern nations. This is certainly a policy that those in government are increasingly eager to explore. They are also keen to develop Moscow as a regional financial centre. At the 2011 Goldman Sachs BRIC conference, Andrey Kostin, the president and CEO of VTB, one of the two most powerful Russian banks, told me that he saw Russia becoming an important centre for financial trading for the former Soviet republics.

There is much that Russia needs to sort out in order to improve its chances of success and to reach the 2050 scenario we have laid out. There are likely to be plenty of opportunities for them to see how well they are doing.

At some stage oil prices will probably fall sharply again. If oil prices fell to $15 a barrel and stayed there, that would almost certainly be a nightmare for Russia, at least in the short term. The sharp drop in oil prices in 2008 to around $30 shows how vulnerable economically Russia can quickly become. But ultimately, actions to force Russia to become less dependent on high oil prices would be good for the country, and force it to develop a real economic base, not one purely dependent on selling its natural resources. Before the 2008 crisis, Russia outperformed our expectations because of the price of oil. Smart policymakers would have known the reasons for its growth and prepared for what came next.

In early 2008, just before the crisis hit Russia, I visited the country to deliver a presentation on Russian growth prospects up to 2020. It turned out my projections were only half as optimistic as the internal Russian numbers. I could sense some irritation in my audience. During the ensuing discussion, I told them: 'You've just had seven years of BRIC life in which oil prices have gone up fivefold. I can guarantee they won't go up fivefold over the next seven years.' Within three months, oil prices had halved and Russian GDP plummeted. It was obvious to me that this was going to happen at some point. What's not clear yet is whether Russia drew the right lessons from the experience.

Russia has to improve its infrastructure too. Like Brazil, Russia is soon to host both an Olympics (the Winter Olympics in Sochi in 2014) and the FIFA World Cup (in 2018). As with Brazil, these sporting events offer Russia a chance to show itself off to the world, as China did in 2008, and to make progress in those simple areas of life that to many are the most important. St Petersburg, for example, is Russia's second largest city and one of the most architecturally beautiful places I have ever visited. Yet I am shocked when I go there each year at the crowding and disorganization at the airport. It recalls the Soviet era. If Russia is ever going to become really successful, surely its airports and other infrastructure must improve.

When I attended the Champions League Final in Moscow in 2008, to see Manchester United play Chelsea, I flew in privately with a group including several Chelsea fans and my son, an avid United supporter. We had been warned that due to the number of people coming in and out of the city, the public flights would be chaotic. We had a great time enjoying

Moscow before the game, which ended happily, after penalties, in the right result: a United victory. We celebrated through the night before blearily heading for our early flight home. Fourteen hours after boarding, we were still sitting on the tarmac, along with a couple of dozen other private planes. The twelve of us on the plane never imagined we would have such an opportunity to get to know one another so well! Frustrated by the lack of information, four of us eventually took a car and travelled to the other side of Moscow and boarded onto the scheduled BA flight at 6.40 a.m. the following morning. Our original flight took off shortly afterwards. It was an expensive and exhausting trip, and an eye-opener into some of Russia's issues.

During our long wait, my travelling companions asked me why on earth there was an R in BRICs, and I have to say that trip had me wondering. At various times we heard that the airport simply couldn't cope with so many flights. Or that President Putin had closed the air space over Moscow so he could visit one of the former Soviet republics and return the same day. Whatever the truth, it was a reminder that in certain mystifying ways Russia is yet to behave with the transparency and efficiency of a fully developed country. We still don't know to this day why we were kept waiting!

I realize that it's wrong to draw too many conclusions from a single experience and I have been to Russia a number of times without experiencing such difficulties. There is also a danger with Russia, as with all the BRICs, of letting our Western biases affect our views of its progress. Provided we remind ourselves of Russia's past, then our judgements of its present and our forecasts for its future will be more grounded in reality.

INDIA

India is the greatest mystery among the BRICs.

Its demographics are astonishing, the most favourable in the world. Over the next twenty-five or thirty years, its working population might increase by the same number of people as currently live in the United States, 300 million. Its population in 2011 is already 1.2 billion and by 2050 could reach 1.7 billion, that's 10–20 per cent more than China's and with far more young people. It would make India's labour force almost as large as the combined labour forces of China and the United States. These are irresistible facts and alone will make India one of the biggest influences on the world.

India also has the great advantages of a credible legal system, many English-language speakers and home-grown technology companies which are expanding globally. It has been provoked to action by the rapid growth of China and has no desire to be left behind by its largest neighbour. In theory, India could overtake Japan in the next 20–30 years to become the third largest economy in the world and, given its demographics, has the potential to increase its real GDP faster than any of the other BRICs. By 2050, India could be more than thirty times bigger than it is today in economic terms. However, of the four BRICs India has the lowest growth environment scores, a fact many visitors would find surprising. But such is the scale of the challenge for India that when people propose I drop the R from BRICs, I point out that for all its faults, on a broad list of variables for sustainable growth, such as our GES, Russia seems stronger than India. I believe India is the most vibrant, beautiful, creative, inspiring place that I have ever seen. But the scale of the poverty is astonishing, and the difficulties of getting things done are equally so.

I will never forget my first trip to Mumbai. As my plane landed I looked out and saw the slums pressing up to the edge of the runway, stretching out for miles. After passing through the airport, an adventure in itself, the journey into town was remarkable. It was night, and seeing so many bodies asleep in the street, my first thought was that they were dead.

By day, Mumbai is an endless traffic jam. Child beggars bang on the car and demand money. It is like living theatre. Despite the appalling poverty, there is an excitement about this vast, limitless city. I love the fact that every time I visit Mumbai, people have different estimates of its population. The official tally is 15 million, but several people tell me it is twice that. I have walked around Mumbai's slums with the people in charge of slum clearance and development who tell me the most extraordinary stories. In their efforts to clear the slums, the city authorities offered people apartments in new, suburban developments. Many would take up the offer but within weeks, lacking any sense of deep community and friendship, would leave their new homes and return to the slums and build a new shack for themselves and their family. You can read some fabulous books about life in Mumbai and Delhi, but there is nothing like visiting.

Contradictions abound concerning India. At Goldman we only started to think seriously about the country after we started the BRIC analysis. It wasn't until our first 2050 scenario was published in 2003 that we considered employing a full-time India economist. In this sense the BRIC concept led us to India rather than the other way round. Our 2050 projections for India certainly took me and others aback. Both inside and outside India, people were stunned by the scale of our projections.

The good news story about India over the past ten years is that it hasn't had a major economic crisis. It hasn't done anything either spectacularly positive or negative. In vital areas, it remains fifteen or twenty years behind China. Urbanization is one good example. There are lots of new cities sprouting up all over India, and in Delhi and Mumbai you can see the infrastructure improving. But the pace isn't always quick. I remember having to drive from Delhi to a satellite town called Gurgaon, a booming technology centre, to meet an advisor to the Indian government. My meeting was scheduled for 9 a.m. and I was keen to be on time. My driver said it would take anywhere between forty-five minutes and two hours. I decided to assume the worst. The trip ended up taking two and a half hours. Within minutes of leaving my hotel, we were stuck in traffic. They were building a new motorway, and as they did so, the existing one had been reduced to one lane, where we jostled with carts and animals as well as other cars. There were hundreds of construction workers doing nothing as far as I could tell, scores of police trying to create order out of the mayhem. I remember sitting in the car with animals pressing in on the sides staring at these beautiful skyscrapers off in the distance. Here were lots of symbols both of India's economic progress and of its dangers all in one anecdote.

I told myself that I would return here on future visits and use this journey as an indicator of India's progress. The new road was eventually finished and the journey from Delhi to Gurgaon now takes half an hour. The Delhi subway and airport were also upgraded on time.

Indian politicians have the will to pull their country forward, but there are moments when I think they want to frustrate this process, as if they are not completely convinced that economic growth is a good thing. Among Indian elites, I often find a resentment of Western practices, development among them. Some simply don't want this vast change. Not long ago, I was attending a meeting in Simla as part of a UK–India Round Table. I got into a big argument with a well-known Indian philosopher, who told me that economic growth only causes damage. He talked about pollution and the dangers of financial markets. Both can be consequences of growth, of course. But I told him that what I felt he was really saying was that he didn't want any of his fellow Indians to escape poverty.

As I have said, I believe keeping control of inflation should be at the core of BRIC macroeconomic policy. There is no better, simpler, clearer way of showing people what is driving government thinking. But Indian politicians tell me that inflation targeting is too complicated, that creating a consumer price index is too difficult and that anyway the volatility of food prices makes it unreliable. I wonder if these are the real reasons, or if it's because some Indian leaders would rather government policy remained a mystery. They don't want it to seem clear.

India has other problems China doesn't have. Its regions are very autonomous, so central government cannot dictate policy. It is a democracy, with all that entails: bickering parties, an antiquated caste system, competing faiths, not to mention a complicated colonial heritage. There are clashing voices and opinions in India, not the single purpose that is present in China. This is not a judgement about the relative merits of democracy and Chinese communism as political

systems, merely an observation about the differences in economic policy as implemented in the two countries.

From an investment perspective, I was worried about India
in 2010 and 2011. Equity market valuations were very high.
For most of the past few years in fact India has traded at a
premium, partly I think because of its very positive potential
and image overseas. People see all these Indian billionaires
and think that's the whole story. Some Indian companies and
individuals have taken advantage of this mispricing to float
their companies and use the capital they raise to buy Western
equivalents at half the price. Some very astute investors
believe that India is a more balanced GDP story than the
popular perception of it allows. They believe that its economy is not so dependent on the rest of the world. This makes
it more resilient in the face of crises elsewhere, and an excellent defensive investment play. If you're worried about the
world economy blowing up, these people believe that you
should invest in India, because its economy is driven by its
own consumption, not exports or foreign investment. It is a
much more self-sufficient economy than those of the other
BRICs. Evidence of this is that over the past decade we have
seen India bear the brunt of rising commodity prices. It has
weathered this just as Brazil weathered the economic crisis
and falling commodity prices. If you are comparing the four
BRICs, you could say that it was impossible to judge the
strength of the growth in Russia and Brazil until commodity
prices fell. Inversely, India has shown its robustness by growing even as a net commodity importer in a decade of ever
rising commodity prices.

Almost every person I know who does business in India,
Indian or not, from the most powerful on down, complains

about the slow bureaucracy. Ordinary permits and approvals can take months to come through, gumming up even the simplest procedures.

I recently heard about a proposed meeting for a visiting UK minister with some Indian officials. The minister's staff were rather baffled when asked if this would be the first time the minister had met one particular Indian official, as if not it would have to be the last. According to the Indian civil service, only two meetings with people of the minister's stature were permitted; the official would not be allowed to meet a foreign politician formally a third time, which seems more than a touch bureaucratic.

India attracts the least foreign investment of the BRICs partly because of this mystifying bureaucracy. If India were ever to allow Tesco or Walmart into the country, it would undoubtedly improve productivity in retail and reduce agricultural waste. But the politicians worry about the effect on Indian society, so they revert to protectionism and block foreign companies.

Reflective of this, to the surprise of many in the West, who are used to meeting highly educated and tech-savvy Indians, India has poor growth environment scores for both technology use and education. At the top end of its educational system, India produces large numbers of well-trained, English-speaking technical graduates, who have driven the success of its service industries. They are also highly computer literate. The vast bulk of its population, however, remains uneducated with very limited access to technology. Hundreds of millions have little or no formal education. The difference between government statistics and reality is large, but it is believed that 20 per cent of children aged between six and fourteen do not attend school at all, and that the dropout rate is high. India's literacy rates are by far the lowest of the BRICs, with female literacy lower than 50 per cent. India struggles at all levels of the education ladder, from primary through tertiary. Any list of the world's top universities these days would probably include many from China, but one at best from India. The Indian government has promised to make large investments at every level of education and must do so simply to meet domestic demand for an educated workforce. By 2020 it hopes to have quadrupled the number of universities.

My personal interest in educational charities has allowed me to meet those with similar interests in India and these discussions have given me further reason for hope. There are many exciting initiatives. These include Pratham, founded in 1994 with the help of UNICEF to make sure more Indian children go to school, and Teach for India, an offshoot of the UK's TeachFirst, which sends recent graduates from Britain's top universities to teach in secondary schools in deprived areas. For India to have any chance of achieving its remarkable potential, educational standards and opportunities have to be increased dramatically.

This is also a business opportunity: for example education-related businesses could become a major export for the UK. Another initiative we discuss at the UK–India Round Table is to 'offshore' the better Western universities. If I were in charge of one of these universities, I would be spending a lot of time exploring opening a 'branch' in the most densely populated urban corners of India.

Just as with charitable educational initiatives, if I were a technology entrepreneur, I would be looking at ways of helping India's poorest to get access to basic technology. Access to the internet and mobile telephones, paired with education, will really help India to get moving. Add this to India's rapid urbanization, and it is easy to imagine its real GDP growth rate rising above that of China. It would also be easy to imagine India having over a decade of 10 per cent growth or more. Failure to invest in education and technology, though, could leave India staggering along as it did from the 1950s until the 1980s, limited by protectionist, interventionist and socialist governments to what was disparagingly called the 'Hindu rate of growth', a dismal 3.5 per cent a year.

As well as targeting inflation the Indian government has several macro and micro issues on its hands.[5] It is not nearly as open to international trade as it should be. This has been a long-standing problem for India. Manmohan Singh, the prime minister since 2009 and an academic economist, wrote his doctoral thesis at Oxford in 1962 about India's export trends and the role they would play in his country's growth. In 1991, when he was appointed finance minister at the urging of the International Monetary Fund, India's trade-to-GDP ratio was a paltry 15 per cent. Thanks to Singh's reforms and the boom in global trade it has improved to over 35 per cent. The country has built new export sectors in services and manufacturing, from energy, pharmaceuticals and gems to the widely familiar IT outsourcing.

Since 2000 in particular, Indian trade with the rest of the world has ballooned. Its share of world exports has risen from 0.6 per cent in 1993 to 1.5 per cent in 2010. As 2011 unfolds, Indian exports continue to rise sharply. After having risen by nearly 40 per cent to $246 billion, easily outstripping government forecasts, exports grew by more than 50 per cent in the first few months of the 2011–12 fiscal year. The Congress Party-led government dreams of $500 billion in annual export revenues within three years, representing growth of 30 per cent a year. Indian exports are in the process of a large-scale rebalancing. As I write this in 2011, just 13 per cent of its exports go to the United States compared to 21 per cent in 2000. Two-thirds of Indian exports now go to markets other than the US and the European Union, mainly to Asia and several African countries.

Amid all this excitement, though, one should recall that Indian exports are rising from a very low base. There is much more trade that India can do, particularly with its neighbours. Along its northern borders are China, a fellow BRIC, and Pakistan, a country with close to 200 million people. Because of their tense political relationship, India and Pakistan scarcely speak to each other, let alone trade. To the north-east is Bangladesh, a country with more than 100 million people. If India's leaders could only shed their fears of free trade, they could propose a free trade area in the subcontinent by 2020. Increased trade between India and Pakistan may even turn out to be the key to ending their mutual hostility. I am always shocked in India by the disdain for Pakistan and told I am naïve for imagining free trade could be the answer. But as a European I look at the way France and Germany – fierce foes in two world wars during the twentieth century – are now partners at the heart of the European Monetary Union. Their intention never to fight again drove them together economically. India and Pakistan might one day be the same.

India and China are showing marked progress in their trading relationship. In 2010, China promised to buy more Indian goods in an attempt to reduce its trading surplus with India. Corporate data suggests that this is working as China buys ever more iron ore, cars and pharmaceuticals from its neighbour. Even so, India's bilateral trade with China was worth just $56 billion in 2010, compared to $80 billion with the European Union.

The rest of the world certainly seems enthused about India. In 2010, President Barack Obama of the United States, Prime Minister David Cameron of the United Kingdom and President Nicolas Sarkozy of France all led large delegations to India. Businesses in their countries are extremely excited about India's prospects. India's trade officials, led by the commerce minister, Anand Sharma, are among the most active in the world these days, travelling all over the Middle East, Africa and Latin America, as well as Europe and Asia, to strike bilateral deals. The world is responding. In Britain Chancellor George Osborne said in 2010 that 'India's policies of trade and investment liberalization are reintegrating it into the world economy, allowing it to regain an influence it had three centuries ago'.

There is still plenty of work for India to do. It remains far too low on the World Bank's indices for ease of doing business, anti-corruption and transparency. According to the World Bank's rankings, anyone trying to export goods from India must file eight documents over an average of seventeen days for each shipment. Contrast this with Singapore, where just four documents are filed over five days. India's infrastructure requires colossal levels of investment, and a more evolved public and corporate bond market to fund it. It also needs to bring down barriers to imports and foreign direct investment.

Its imports are rising, but its politicians remain far too worried about foreign competition and cutting tariffs. To achieve its potential, India needs to import a lot, whether it is Australian and Indonesian natural resources or British education. The easier it makes this process, the faster it can grow. Improving its infrastructure and health-care systems will be essential to boosting everything about India's future.

Foreign investors may be eager to get involved in India, but they are scared off by rules and legal threats which make it hard for them to take significant stakes in Indian companies. India's political leaders understand the need for foreign direct investment to stimulate growth, but seem frightened by the popular reaction to admitting more foreigners to their markets.

Agriculture and retail are two glaring areas which could benefit from foreign expertise and investment. Walmart, Tesco and Carrefour have been keen to enter the Indian market for years, but have been barred from doing so in any meaningful way. A powerful group of middlemen, who link farmers to Indian consumers through tens of millions of small shops and pushcarts, have persuaded politicians not to let in the big Western chains. Their participation has been limited to offering technical support to Indian retailers. What may finally be changing this attitude are persistently high food prices. Foreign companies could wring stupendous efficiencies from India's food supply chain, reducing waste and lowering prices, through simple advances such as better refrigerated transport. But it remains to be seen whether the politicians have the nerve to take on the traders who prosper under the existing system, taking commissions from farmers and pushing up prices for consumers without offering much in the way of supply-chain improvement.

I once discussed this with a senior official in India's Finance Ministry, who told me bluntly that the battle over Tesco and Walmart had nothing to do with growth, but with the risk of Indians losing their jobs. Such short-term thinking is regrettable: admitting foreign investment would undoubtedly improve the consumer experience for Indians and enhance the efficiency and productivity of its agricultural industry.

The more I travel to India and think about its challenges, the more I find myself concluding that, as with so many issues in life, its problem is one of state of mind. The problems of raising educational standards and achievement, spreading the use of technology, boosting trade and foreign investment, increasing agricultural productivity, all boil down to one issue: leadership. It is perhaps as simple and as difficult as this. India must wrestle in so many areas to change and advance, because it is such a complex nation to lead and govern.

I find the contrast to China so illuminating: two countries with similar populations and yet China, in theory at least still a communist country, strides ahead while India, the world's biggest democracy, often struggles.

CHINA

On my first visit to Beijing in 1990, I arrived via what was also my first ever trip to Taiwan. I remember thinking I had it all the wrong way round. Taiwan, a democracy, seemed more like a communist country, its capital Taipei all tall, grey buildings and order. In contrast, walking around the streets near my hotel in Beijing, I found street markets and lots of people buying and selling. It was the first time I sensed that Chinese communism wasn't anything like my vision of it living in the West. My idea of communism had been very much shaped by the Soviet Union. On that first trip, the communism I saw on the streets of Beijing seemed nothing like the evil tyranny I was expecting. There was more subtlety and nuance to this story.

I love travelling to China and sharing its people's optimism. It's a change from the cynicism and negativity I hear constantly in the West, where people seem to have lost their excitement about the future. I love being in a place surrounded by 1.3 billion people yearning and striving for more than what they have. People tell me from time to time that I should consider taking the C out of BRICs because China is of such huge relevance on its own. Of course some say that if I took the C out of BRICs there would be no story about the others. They have a point. China is the greatest story of our generation. I've visited China more times than I've visited the other three BRICs put together.

There is simply no overstating China's importance to all of us, not just to 1.3 billion Chinese. The entire planet, all 6.5 billion of us, is invested in China's success. When I joined Goldman Sachs in 1995, China's economy was worth around $500 billion. It has grown more than tenfold in just fifteen years, averaging more than 10 per cent real GDP growth throughout that period. By 2001, China's GDP was around $1.5 trillion, smaller than that of the United Kingdom or France. Now it dwarfs both, and in 2010 overtook Japan to become the second largest economy in the world. It could conceivably continue to grow at close to 10 per cent in the decade up to 2020, the way it did between 2000 and 2010. I suspect it will get harder to sustain quite this degree of growth and it may be better for it to slow down somewhat as policymakers focus more on the quality of growth rather than just the sheer quantity. It will certainly be critical for all of us. We might worry often about the debt crises in the eurozone, but anything that happens in China is far more important to the fate of the world economy.

Like all the BRICs, China is rife with contradictions, and no experience captures these better than a visit to Mao's mausoleum in Tiananmen Square in Beijing. A friend of mine, a journalist for *The Times*, told me that if I wanted to understand modern China I had to pay a visit. It was like going to a football match, with thousands of poor Chinese crowding around, pushing and spitting on the ground. It was a little scary at first. The police herd you and you worry you might get trampled. Near the entrance is a shop where you can buy flowers for 3 renminbi. So many were buying a bunch to present before the embalmed body of China's Great Helmsman. As we came to the mausoleum, we saw banks of flowers rising up around Mao. But then I noticed a man picking up the flowers and taking them back round to the store to resell them. So we had huge crowds coming to pay their respects to a man who authorized the killing of millions of people, and buying flowers knowing they would be resold the moment they had laid them down.

Capitalism, communism and Chinese ancestor worship were all being practised in one crowded spot in the heart of Beijing. Within a few hundred yards of the mausoleum there is a Lamborghini showroom, where China's new rich buy sports cars with cash. If you can process this mass of confusing images, then you have a chance of understanding modern China.

In our 2003 paper forecasting the growth of the BRICs, we predicted that China would be the biggest economy in the world by 2039. Professor Niall Ferguson, now at Harvard, was one of the many who ridiculed us. He said our projections were some of the silliest things he had read. Like many others then and since, he assumed that we expected China to just extrapolate past growth. We didn't do that. (I have got to know Niall well since. Of course, he has changed his mind, although I am not sure it is anything to do with me.) China, we wrote, does not have to keep growing at 10 per cent for its GDP to pass the size of the United States. It can grow at more modest rates and still become number one.

Since then we have changed the period in which China might challenge the US on a couple of occasions. In 2008 we said that China could become the world's largest economy by 2027. A few months later *The Economist* one-upped us, saying China might overtake the United States by 2020. To achieve this it would have to grow by 10 per cent a year all the way to 2020, which is possible but unlikely. If the renminbi were to appreciate against the US dollar at an even faster rate than it has been doing, so that the dollar value of any Chinese growth would be greater, then it could happen on paper, but it will be tough for it to occur quite that soon. At the end of 2010, China was still only about one-third the size of the US in comparable US-dollar terms.

We deliberately called our 2003 paper 'Dreaming with BRICs' partly to make it clear that our projections carried no guarantee, but also to encourage people to consider the likelihood that China and the other BRICs could ascend to challenge the G7's worldwide economic supremacy and influence. Eight years on, the idea that China might become the world's biggest economy is more widely accepted.

The first people in the West to understand the China story were the international business people, those who ran multinational corporations, the big brands of retail, product and communications empires. They went to China frequently and could see what was happening on the ground. But the changes should have been apparent to any regular visitor. When I first visited China in the early 1990s, I was one of the few people being picked up from the airport in Beijing in a black limousine. Most of the traffic going into the city was bicycles and carts. I vividly remember having to stop and wait in the car after two of these bike-powered carts collided and fruit and vegetables were thrown all over the road. The last section of the seventy-odd-kilometre road to Badaling, where the Great Wall comes closest to Beijing, used to be a dirt track. On a more recent visit I went to Badaling with my wife, and the dirt track had become a highway. We stayed at a boutique hotel right beside the Wall. When I first visited, Beijing had one giant ring road looping around the city. Today it has eight, the outermost running close by the Great Wall.

The key, of course, to China's extraordinary growth has been its population. Once its government decided to engage with the rest of the world in the early 1980s, this triggered the economic changes which gathered ever more pace in the 1990s and 2000s. Millions moved into cities, contributing to and benefiting from China's surge as a global manufacturer. As we found out, though, in 2008, the world couldn't really cope with this status quo any more. And from a global perspective, just having the world's largest population might not be enough. They also need to be the right people.

As I discussed in Chapter 2, a large working population boosting its productivity is the key recipe for achieving persistent stronger growth. China does have some challenges in this regard. Its working population is ageing and may soon peak, which could land China with the kind of challenges faced by Italy, Japan and perhaps Russia. In April 2011, China released its 2010 national census, which reported that excluding Hong Kong and Macau its total population was 1.34 billion, an increase of about 74 million from the last census taken in 2000. It has been growing by just 0.6 per cent a year since 2000, compared to 1.1 per cent a year between 1990 and 2000. While the head of the National Bureau of Statistics bullishly attributed the slowdown to China's one-child policy, this highlights a more troubling aspect. The number of young people is falling sharply. Only 16.6 per cent of the population is under fourteen, around half the number of twenty years earlier. At the same time the number over sixty-five years old is 9 per cent, nearly twice the figure of twenty years ago. If China were to follow the same trend over the next twenty years its demographics would change dramatically, with its working-age population dropping and its GDP growth rate slowing abruptly. China's growth rate will not be as strong in the future as it has been in the past twenty years.

It will slow: it is just a matter of by how much and how smoothly. The government announced a lower target of around 7 per cent for real GDP growth in its twelfth five-year plan, starting in 2012. Its previous five-year plan aimed for 7.5 per cent real GDP growth, though it turned out to be closer to 11 per cent. It is unlikely that the gap between the target and the actual outcome in the next five years will be as wide. Government assumptions for the five-year growth target are just broad desires, not hard targets, but for the current administration to assume a lower target is recognition of some of their challenges, and possibly reflects a desire for somewhat softer, better-quality growth.

No demographics are definite. Rising wealth may lead to improved health, longer life expectancy and a desire for more children. There are already signs that the government appears to be relaxing the one-child policy in the more prosperous urban areas, notably Shanghai and Beijing, where families with more than one child are a fairly common sight. In a number of areas it seems that provided you can pay for a second child, you can have one, especially if the first child is a girl, given China's shortage of women.

China might also be able to make up for its population slowdown in other ways. According to the census, the ratio of Chinese citizens living in urban areas has risen from 36.2 per cent to just below 50 per cent. If other advanced economies are any guide, there are still another 260 million Chinese, or 20 per cent of the population, yet to move into cities. This is almost the equivalent of urbanizing the entire population of the United States. As I have written, I believe urbanization has a great positive effect on GDP growth, as people compete to improve their lives and share knowledge at a swifter rate.

In any case, growth is also about the productivity of those working, not just the fact that they work. The number of Chinese people receiving a tertiary education is rising quickly, which should also lead to stronger growth. The remarkable speed at which Chinese researchers are starting to be among the most successful scientists and engineers in the world is a strong sign that productivity in key areas is on the rise. As China urbanizes more of its people, boosting their productivity, perhaps also helping their individual flexibility and creativity, will be vital.

With some continued modest appreciation of the renminbi, by 2050 Chinese GDP could be worth $70 trillion, with GDP per capita around $50,000, around twelve times its 2011 level. The Chinese would still be far from being the world's wealthiest people, but at this level of GDP China would certainly have the most billionaires.

*

Our opinion in the 2003 paper that China could one day be the world's largest economy sent many Westerners into a spin and is still not universally accepted, despite subsequent experience. The world has become so used to American economic dominance that the idea of another country, let alone a communist one, taking its place is unsettling to some. But it is worth asking: what difference would it actually make? China has long had the world's largest population, so it shouldn't be that surprising that it could also have the world's largest economy. Indeed, it has been the biggest economy before, albeit many centuries ago, so why not at some stage in the future? Luxembourg does not complain about having a smaller economy than Germany, so why should the rest of us worry about China? What do we find so frightening about the idea of China reaching its economic potential?

The first anxiety is political. Most in the West are conditioned to mistrust any form of authoritarian rule. The Chinese, evidently, do not feel the same way. Provided their government delivers rising prosperity, they seem accepting of its current form. My own hunch is that whether China ultimately becomes a democracy is less important than whether it evolves into a more open version of what it is today, allowing people the rights corresponding with their greater wealth. Byron Wien, vice chairman of Advisory Services at the Blackstone Group, wrote an amusing account of a visit to India and China in the spring of 2011, during which he asked a group of Chinese people how they felt about not being able to vote. One of them told him: 'What's the big deal about voting? In the US everyone can do it and only half the people do. If voting were that great a thing, like sex for example, everyone would do it.'

The second reason for the West's anxiety about China's ascent is its reluctance to recognize its own importance. Its leaders are so focused on their internal problems that they show little interest in shaping world affairs. Like the former colonial powers, they go to Africa to sign commodities deals, but it is not obvious that the reason they do so is because they care about Africans. There is some evidence that the United States was similarly loath to accept the global role befitting its economic status in the first half of the twentieth century. It took the Second World War to really drag it out of its shell. It is the case today that China is more focused on China than on its external responsibilities, which is not what others would perhaps want. I expect this to change as it achieves more sustained progress and advancement.

Thirdly, many seem to believe that China's gain must mean the West's loss. This is just not true. (I return to this apparently thorny issue later in Chapter 7.) China's long-term sustainable growth has nothing to do with where its GDP stands in relation to that of the United States. International trade means that both the US and China will benefit from China's rise.

A glance at China's growth environment scores reveals why. Its general macroeconomic scores are promising. China scores well for its stable inflation rate, its external financial position, government debt, investment levels and openness to foreign trade. On the micro side, China also exceeds the average for big developing countries. The only two areas where it falls just below the average are corruption and in some areas concerning the use of technology. The latter is undoubtedly changing quickly.

It is distinctly possible that China's GDP will never overtake that of the US. In the 1980s it seemed Japan was destined to become the world's largest economy. Its companies were storming the world, its investors buying the Rockefeller

Center in New York and setting new price records for Impressionist paintings. Rather than being signs of strength, however, these turned out to be omens of Japan's asset bubble. Once that imploded, Japan embarked on two decades and counting of deflation. There are many who look at the frothy prices of Chinese real estate and say China is heading for a similar fate.

Like the Japanese in the 1980s, the Chinese have also been reluctant to let their currency float. The Japanese kept the yen artificially low to protect their manufacturing export sector. The Americans had to threaten to shut Japanese products out of the US market before Japan allowed the yen to rise. A similar situation could arise with China, which until 2005 was keeping the renminbi artificially low. If US industrial production shows no sign of substantial recovery in coming years and unemployment remains high, while China continues its apparently strong growth, the US could threaten to ban Chinese goods, which would leave Chinese exports facing a huge slowdown.

While there are some grounds for thinking that China could fail for similar reasons as Japan, I tend to doubt such simple comparisons. There are some very big differences too. Japan seems even today, after the tragic earthquake of 2011, a more formal and closed society. In the past on many visits to Tokyo I used to stay at the Okura Hotel, next door to the American embassy. To use the hotel gym, you'd have to sign in with one person, receive your gym uniform from another and be shown in by a third – you worked as hard to get in as you did once inside. The Japanese attention to detail has always been fantastic, but the flip side is a large waste of human resources in the service sector. The English language is hardly ever used in Japan and it is consequently tricky to get around the place.

The Chinese, by contrast, are doing much more to communicate with the outside world, whether it is in business, politics or tourism. I am constantly impressed by the people I meet when I visit China. An obvious contrast to Japan for a Western visitor is that so many Chinese speak English or are rapidly acquiring the skill, so we can converse without a translator. Visitors appreciate the way the Chinese are so eager to communicate. You can experience it in many aspects of life. A couple of years ago, my wife and I were bicycling along the Yulong river near Guilin, and as we entered a small village I noticed a big billboard on a dilapidated wall which read 'Success in English equals success in life'. There in one simple message was all of China's eagerness to embrace another language as a means to achieve its ambitions. It points to a broader willingness to engage with the world, and not hide behind a closed, cultural identity. This is one of the most powerful illustrations I have seen on my many trips and has such important resonance for all of us, the world over.

Another thing that impresses me is how worried the Chinese are that everything could go wrong. Normally, it's my job to worry. But the Chinese, I'm delighted to say, do a lot of my worrying for me. They seem constantly worried. A couple of years ago, I was giving a talk to a group of mid-level policymakers and regulators. Afterwards, three of them came up to me and asked if I was worried about a property bubble in China. This was exactly the fear expressed by many Western investors, and I was pleased to see the Chinese took it just as seriously. This was very different from Japan in the late 1980s, when policymakers refused to acknowledge the bubble building up in almost every asset class in the country. The Japanese policymaking machine at the time was in complete denial about the problems which have since held the country back. In a similar spirit, ten years ago the Chinese knew that their banking system needed to evolve. So they appointed a commission made up of six eminent banking specialists from around the world to advise them. This willingness to reach out, to address problems as they emerge, this practical, realistic approach I find refreshing in China.

It was fascinating reading the news reports about the ninetieth anniversary of the Communist Party of China in the summer of 2011. The Chinese are very proud of the fact that they don't make judgements about how other nations behave, that they focus on themselves and their internal stability and prosperity. Critics might say that China does not judge others for fear of being judged itself. This may be right. But what I see is a set of leaders determined to look clinically at their challenges and address them without prejudice.

China's challenges, like everything else about the country, are monumental. I've seen rivers choked with rubbish. I've been in Beijing on days when it has been impossible to see the sun because of the pollution. In Shanghai one hears of people dying of illnesses related to the polluted environment. And this is just what the occasional visitor picks up on.

Another popular criticism of China is that investment spending is too high, too unprofitable and thus unsustainable, as it was in Japan in the 1980s. Compared to almost any other economy, the share of reported investment in China's GDP does seem high. For the sake of balanced growth, the commonly held view is that private consumption should rise as a share of GDP and relative to investment. But it is not so straightforward.

Firstly, there are significant doubts about the accuracy of Chinese official data. China's national accounts are frequently revised to reveal an economy bigger than officially reported in the past. My old economics colleagues in Hong Kong have expressed significant doubts about how the investment data are collated. They believe that the government's counting of data ends up overestimating the size of official investment and underestimates the size of services expenditure in relation to the overall economy and as a share of GDP. If so, the accurate and truer share of investment spending as a percentage of GDP is being overestimated in the official numbers.

A related oft-quoted concern among hedge fund investors and others is that China fiddles its economic data out of malice or a desire to misrepresent reality. I can't see any reason for the government to do this. We need to check our own biases before questioning China's data accuracy or tarring China's investment spending as unprofitable. UK GDP data often strike me as less accurate even than China's, but do people question that? The Chinese may simply not share the short-term view of profitability we have in the West.

Given China's political and social structure, it is more likely that the success or failure of the investment build-up in the past years will only be judged over the next decade or so. Much of the investment has gone into infrastructure. Is the recently expanded Beijing airport a good investment or bad? Is it more wasteful than the investment in Terminal 5 at Heathrow? Or comparable terminal extensions in US airports which, I believe, have often added little to the ease and comfort of travel? As someone who flies frequently, I would suggest that the expanded Beijing airport is a positive initiative. Similarly, while many of China's new roads outside the major urban cities are traffic free, they are very unlikely to stay that way. As I mentioned earlier, 50 per cent of China's population now live in cities, and another 20 per cent are likely to follow: another 260 million people needing housing and transport infrastructure. I already hear stories that Beijing airport is not big enough, despite the fact that it was only expanded in 2008. When you live in London and see how difficult it is for Heathrow to add a runway, or suffer the daily challenge of the M25 motorway which encircles the city, you wonder whether the UK might not profitably use some of China's approach to infrastructure investment.

Yes, there are buildings standing empty, but I don't share the concerns expressed by many about them, for they will eventually be filled as the Chinese urbanize. If China were closer to 70 per cent urbanized, I would be a lot more worried about the notion of excessive investment: as China urbanizes more the pace of investment needs to slow. As things stand, though, China's investments have set it up for more growth, and it has achieved this without so far succumbing to crippling inflation or destroying its balance of payments, and it seems set to continue.

Many of the same points could be made about fears of a Chinese property crash. Jim Chanos, an American hedge fund manager and famed short-seller, is a well-known pessimist regarding the economic outlook for China. He has called its property bubble 'Dubai times 1000 – or worse'.[6] I can't think of an odder comparison. China remains far from fully urbanized and there seems to be huge latent demand for housing. Dubai's internal population is tiny and watching their bubble develop made it a lot easier to question. China's leaders plan for the future and are ahead of their population when it comes to housing and infrastructure, so at times there will seem to be excess capacity, but it is soon filled up. Visitors to Beijing will often talk of the empty office blocks. But

I have seen empty office blocks in China for years, and they quickly fill up.

If I choose to be paranoid, I look at the fact that urbanization of China's youth is now reaching 60 per cent, closer to capacity than the national average. Within six or seven years, there may be no young people left in the countryside. Given China's gender imbalance and low birth rate, that could become a significant problem. If it's true that the countryside is nearly emptied out, urbanization is complete, and there is no one left to fill the housing and offices being built in cities, then I will worry seriously about over-capacity. But someone needs to persuade me that this is the case.

One thing that is impossible to ignore is the fact of fast-rising Chinese wealth. I read in late 2009 that 5 per cent of China's population, or 65 million people, now have incomes of around $35,000 per year, and these are concentrated in the major cities. This would be equivalent to the wealth of a UK or France. If true, it explains property prices in certain areas of Shanghai and Beijing. This affluent new class does not have the range of investments available to their peers in Europe or North America. China's poorly developed financial markets mean that property is often the best of a limited set of investment choices.

Then again, the Chinese government is also taking measures to prevent a crash, and is certainly doing more than the United States government did between 2001 and 2007 to pop its own real-estate bubble. Since 2009 the Chinese have limited the percentage that can be borrowed to buy a second home, and certain cities have imposed other restrictions on speculators. These appear to have taken some of the heat out of the market.

Another recurring issue is China's dependence on exports for economic growth. Certainly in the 1990s and 2000s China took advantage of its low-cost labour to attract multinationals from all over the world, eager to satisfy the insatiable appetite for cheaper consumer goods in the West, and in the US in particular. The surge in China's exports together with buoyant investment has been key to China's remarkable rise over the last two decades. For a brief moment in 2007, China was exporting the equivalent of 12 per cent of its GDP just to the United States. This, of course, was unsustainable. A severe external jolt, such as occurred with the global credit crisis, was bound to knock such an economy off course. Sure enough, China was badly hurt by the downturn in the United States.

But I think that over the long haul, the shock will have done it good, forcing the Chinese to adopt more policies to boost domestic consumption and develop a more balanced economy. China could not depend on growth sustained by exports and public investment as the dominant rising share for ever, and a shift to a model involving broader and stronger domestic consumption has to be a good thing for China, and almost definitely for the rest of us too.

Since 2007 a lot has changed. China's trade surplus has declined sharply: in 2010 it slowed to 3.8 per cent of GDP compared to around 11 per cent in 2007. Moreover, the notion that China grows at the expense of other countries is simply wrong. In 2010, China imported nearly $1.4 trillion worth of goods and services, an increase of $400 billion over the previous year. The US imported $2.3 trillion worth of goods and services in 2010. At the current pace, China's imports could exceed those of the US within five years. When China starts running much lower trade surpluses this will knock the wind out of those critics who blame its exports for the loss of Western jobs and threaten protectionism.

It seems clear that, during the next five years, Chinese policymakers are going to choose quality over quantity of growth. Quality will mean increased private consumption as a share of overall GDP; measures to improve health care and pensions, and the rights of migrant workers in the cities; and improved energy efficiency with a focus on alternative energy, which I will discuss in Chapter 5. At every turn in its story of economic growth, there will be new challenges for China. Imagine being Chinese in 2030, and having seen your wealth quadruple, from $6,000 to $24,000, in just twenty years. Social change will inevitably accompany rising wealth.

In July 2011 two high-speed trains collided in eastern China, killing thirty-five people. This disturbing event was taken by many in the country as a powerful sign that perhaps the Chinese authorities can't rush everything, and the understandable backlash from the middle-class passengers who ride the trains will surely force policymakers to think more carefully about pursuing too many grand projects too quickly in future. When I saw the early response to this accident, it confirmed a growing belief of mine that China is about to enter a new phase of growth, more to do with quality and sustainability.

My broad experiences in business have taught me that problems and crises are inevitable. What matters is how they are dealt with. With regard to its environment, the problem is so severe that the Chinese government is taking equally severe and drastic measures. It is perhaps the most aggressive country in the world in its pursuit of clean technology. China is determined to reduce its use of oil and gas. The major short-term policy issue for China is inflation. Inflation could push China's economy into problems. On a recent trip I had a guide taking me from meeting to meeting. We were talking on our way back to the airport and he started moaning about the rising price of food and apartments. For a Chinese to complain to a foreign stranger means the problem is probably serious. This explains why Chinese policymakers are currently doing a lot to reduce excessive stimulus to the economy, slow the rate of money supply growth and trying to reduce inflation. If they fail, some of the wealth created in recent years will very quickly evaporate and life will be tougher for many.

I recently read an article which said that the Communist Party of China with its 80 million members is not just the world's largest political party but also its biggest chamber of commerce.[7] It pursues its economic interests with remarkable efficiency. Not having to worry about voters, elections or rival parties allows the Chinese government to act with the kind of speed and decisiveness rarely found in a democracy. It does occasionally worry me when I sometimes meet some Chinese corporate types and they seem like government transplants. I get irritated when I hear their speakers rambling on and deviating endlessly from prepared remarks for more than their allotted time. It suggests a dangerous lack of creativity and there might be excessive bureaucracy about the nation and its people. The other BRICs aren't like this. But perhaps it is generational. When I meet young Chinese people and hear them talk and sense their energy then I am back to being optimistic again. I remain as intrigued about China's future as I was that first time I visited Beijing.

4

The New Growth Markets

The arrival as economic forces of the four BRIC economies and other large populous nations has increasingly led me to believe that the world economy is probably stronger and healthier than some might fear. It is not as dependent on the G7 economies as it was in my early days at Goldman Sachs, which, given their challenges, is a relief. The rise of China and the BRICs has not gone unnoticed among other large emerging economies. The remarkable success of China alone has encouraged other countries to explore ways of boosting their prosperity by becoming more engaged with the rest of the world.

Back in 2001 and 2003 many people wondered why we singled out only the four BRIC economies for dramatic growth. This prompted us to explore more closely the growth opportunity for other countries and in our 2005 paper, 'How Solid are the BRICs?' we introduced the 'Next Eleven' or the 'N-11' acronym. It was simply a way to describe the next eleven largest populated emerging economies, and a study of their potential. In particular we tried to gauge whether any of them could become as relevant as the four BRIC economies.

The N-11 grouping is not particularly cohesive, but all eleven are developing countries with large populations and

many would have exciting potential if they were to participate more fully in the global economy. It includes several
contrasting nations: Mexico from Latin America, Turkey on
the edge of Europe and Asia, Egypt and Iran from the Middle
East, Nigeria from Africa, and six countries which span the
whole of Asia – Bangladesh, Indonesia, South Korea, Pakistan, the Philippines and Vietnam.

Mexico and South Korea stood out as OECD members
with by far the highest income levels in the group. Korea in
particular is closer to a developed country than a developing
one, and its GDP per capita and high growth environment
scores reflect that. As a result of their differences from the rest
of the group, it seemed that any projection of the world's
largest economies up to 2050 might well include these two.
Applying the same method to the N-11 as we had for the
BRICs, we projected that by 2050 Mexico's GDP could
make it the world's sixth largest economy, comparable to that
of Russia, and that Indonesia, Nigeria and Korea could overtake Italy and Canada. But aside from Mexico and possibly
Korea, the rest of the N-11 would not contribute to global
economic growth to anything like the degree that the four
BRIC countries will.

In terms of income per capita, we projected that Korea
would overtake every member of the current G7 except the
United States, that Mexico would join Russia in converging
on developed country income levels, and that Turkey, along
with China and Brazil, would have per capita incomes similar to those we see in the United States today. If other N-11
members were to have any chance of catching up with the
developed world, we said that a number of them would have to
rely more on productivity gains because they lacked the vast
populations we see in the BRICs. Some such as Bangladesh,

Indonesia and Nigeria do have powerful demographics and they could see dramatic growth if they get their productivity improving. But even if this were to happen, Bangladesh and Nigeria are currently far too small to catch up with the BRICs in terms of size. Indonesia seems rather better placed, but it too would require strong productivity gains.

Studying the N-11's growth environment scores in 2005, we found a wide range, from Korea, which scored very well, to Nigeria, Pakistan and Bangladesh, which did very poorly. There are countries with specific weaknesses: Vietnam needs to reduce its government deficit, Turkey must improve its technology scores and be more open to international trade, while Iran has a low-scoring political system. Then there are those with broad-based challenges like Egypt, Indonesia, the Philippines, Bangladesh, Nigeria and Pakistan, which under-perform in every area from fiscal discipline to education, investment rates and health care. Even assuming the most optimistic growth paths for the N-11, we concluded that only Korea and Mexico were serious candidates to have a BRIC-like impact on the world.

Though their growth environment scores since 2005 have progressed unevenly, all the N-11 countries have shown a desire to move down the path to growth. They may not succeed but they merit our attention. We were not trying to pick winners when we selected them, but just to try to understand how to assess their actual and potential growth and determine whether they could be as powerful as any of the BRICs.

Looking towards 2050, we identified three different tracks the N-11 countries might follow.[1] The first we believed would apply to Korea, Mexico and Turkey, where incomes and development levels are already reasonably high, growth conditions are decent and the challenge will be to sustain and improve those conditions in order to converge with the world's richest economies. The second track would better suit two other traditionally strong emerging markets, Indonesia and the Philippines, which need to advance further to get closer to the first group. The third track would be for those which have featured on fewer investors' radar, namely Egypt, Nigeria, Pakistan, Bangladesh, Iran and Vietnam.

The countries in this final group, notably Vietnam, Nigeria and Bangladesh, are quite different but they all have interesting potential and merit investor attention. While only a couple of the N-11 have the potential to move into the very largest group of economies, the growth stories of them all are striking.

We looked at the G7 countries, the BRICs and the N-11, and tried to envision them in 2050. What we foresaw were the following groupings: a rich club with per capita incomes of $65,000 per annum or more, made up of Russia, Korea and all the G7 except Italy; an upper-middle-income group with incomes between $40,000 and $65,000, comprising Italy, Mexico, China, Brazil and Turkey; a lower-middle-income group with incomes between $20,000 and $40,000, comprising Vietnam, Iran, Indonesia, Egypt, the Philippines and India; and finally a low-income group with incomes below $20,000, comprising Nigeria, Pakistan and Bangladesh. Thinking like this would help us, and, we hoped, investors and companies, to plan for the future, to see which regions of the world will be growing, how their wealth will advance, to what extent, and how their populations might behave as consumers.

In early 2011 I decided to further refine my view on the world's most dynamic economies. In a paper jointly authored with my colleagues Anna Stupnytska and James Wrisdale, I published new research introducing the idea of 'Growth Markets'.[2] Given the increasing importance of some of these economies, we set out to differentiate them from the traditional emerging market universe. Growth Markets each account for at least 1 per cent of global GDP, which means they have sufficient size and resources to really look after themselves, and importantly have a direct influence on the rest of us. Of the N-11 countries, we identified Indonesia, Mexico, Korea and Turkey as already of sufficient size in terms of GDP, and likely to see their own share of world GDP rise. I now believe these economies, along with the BRICs, should be described as 'Growth Markets'.

Growth Markets are countries which we reckoned had the right demographics and productivity momentum to grow faster than the world average. They also had superior growth environments to most emerging markets, and the financial infrastructure, market size and depth required by international investors. They offered plenty of different, liquid investment opportunities.

N-11 countries which do not qualify today, such as Nigeria, the Philippines, Egypt and Iran, may become Growth Markets over time, as might others such as South Africa. Nigeria and the Philippines may grow to sufficient size by the mid-2040s, and Egypt by 2050. One of them may eventually take the place of Korea, which could soon graduate to developed market status. The Growth Markets concept is intended to help people see the importance of these economies, and to allay their fears about doing business and investing in them.

The simplest way of demonstrating the power of the current Growth Market group is to consider their combined potential nominal GDP growth from 2010 to 2019: around

$16 trillion, or between four and five times the increase in the United States. At least three-quarters of this is likely to come from the BRICs, with half coming from China. Growth in the other four combined will be equivalent to growth in the US or the eurozone. It seems inappropriate and inopportune to keep thinking of these as emerging markets.

Despite some initial misconceptions in the media (see later), the Growth Market grouping was not an expansion of BRICs, but something quite different. My team and I felt that the 'emerging markets' label no longer captured what was going on in key areas of the global economy.

The four BRICs and the N-11 all have large populations. Together they comprise close to 4 billion people, almost two-thirds of the world's population. If they all do things to improve both their productivity and sustainable growth, then they will have a better future – which will be positive for the rest of us.

So what distinguishes all these economies from one another, and how should people think of them?

I have come to define a true BRIC-like economy as one that either is already 5 per cent of global GDP, or has the potential to be that big. Of the four BRICs only China currently satisfies this criterion, although Brazil is getting close now and India and Russia are likely to achieve this in the next decade or soon after.

By contrast, the N-11 is a more diverse grouping. Some are quite advanced, others not. Indeed, seven are still too small, or not advancing rapidly enough, to be defined as anything other than traditional 'emerging markets'. But it is feasible that some might make the leap one day to Growth Markets, if not to BRIC status.

The N-11 has established itself as a defined group in business circles, and is closely watched by investors. Some people seem to think we have created a deeply philosophical notion, but it was literally a phrase we thought up to describe eleven emerging nations that share one common factor: they have a lot of people.

I am occasionally embarrassed by how popular the N-11 concept has become. A number of events and investment ideas have recently focused on the idea. In March 2011 I was asked to attend a major annual conference held on the shores of Lake Como in Italy and to participate in a panel discussing the world economy as well as host a session on the 'Next Eleven', along with various important people from N-11 countries. Unfortunately I couldn't participate as I was invited at short notice to attend another important event in China, but this high-level gathering was yet another indication of how both the N-11 and Growth Market concepts are fast becoming the focus of international interest.

Of the N-11, it seems that Indonesia, Mexico, Turkey and Korea have the most justifiable gripe about not being accorded status equal to the BRICs, but, unwieldy acronym revision aside, none fully satisfies my elementary criteria.

When we introduced the N-11 idea, Mexico seemed the most obvious candidate for inclusion, since I had briefly considered it a potential contender for the original BRIC group. With its sizeable population, I thought it could feasibly become as large as Brazil or Russia by 2050. Now I realize that I was lucky not to include it in the BRICs. It is quite remarkable how modest Mexico's GDP growth has been in the past decade, especially in view of its prowess as an oil producer and the rise in oil prices.

The policymakers of some of the Growth Markets also have aspirations for them to be part of the BRIC world, now that it has become a political club. Indonesia is an oft-discussed candidate. Its policymakers like to tell me about the country's favourable demographics, its large, vibrant young population, its cycle of stronger growth, reasonably stable inflation and the rising wealth and aspirations of its citizens. By 2015 they believe their annual growth rate could rise to 9 per cent, which would merit their inclusion alongside the BRICs.

But I would be impressed if they could continue with their current growth rate of 6 per cent, with the bonus of steady inflation, never mind 9 per cent. The Indonesian economy is currently only about half the size of Russia's or India's, and to become as big as the original BRICs it would need to boost its productivity considerably. It would have to grow dramatically to catch up with Russia in the immediate future, never mind the bigger BRICs, and I can't see how it would meet my definition of reaching at least 5 per cent of world GDP. But clearly Indonesia, along with the other Growth Markets, is becoming much more economically important to the world.

The size and wealth of economies and their growth potential, whether N-11 members or not, can become subjects of endless debate. I have ended up at a simple resting place when I get into these discussions. For any country beyond the original four to become a true BRIC, it needs to have both a large population, evidence of strong growth and a strong GES. Without all of these it will never have a large economy. Of the N-11, Bangladesh, Nigeria and Pakistan all have large populations, but low growth environment scores across most of the components – and they show little signs of dramatic growth.

Some of the other N-11 countries have high GES, but either smaller populations or a small base in terms of current GDP size. South Korea has a higher GES than both Germany and the US, but it is unlikely to become as big as either because it doesn't have enough people. Vietnam has a high GES but has an economy worth less than $100 billion.

Just before we published the paper explaining the concept of Growth Markets in early 2011, I had what I'd mistakenly thought was an off-the-record conversation with a journalist from the *Financial Times*. I woke the following day to read the *FT* headline 'BRICs Creator Adds Newcomers to List'. I knew that the press in the four relevant N-11 countries would push to make something of it; sure enough the following day most Korean media outlets had the story and were calling and emailing for comment.

It was also suggested that Goldman, and I in particular, were trying to create fresh focus and attention in order to attract investment flows, and that my coining of the term 'Growth Markets' was simply a marketing gimmick. The next day the *FT*'s Lex column noted that from the moment I coined the BRIC acronym until the world markets reached a peak in October 2007, the Morgan Stanley Capital International BRIC index, launched in 2005 to track shares in the BRIC markets, gained 625 per cent in US-dollar terms, compared to 499 per cent for emerging markets and 74 per cent for developed stocks. The obvious inference was that my classification had somehow influenced the markets, and that I was now trying to pull off a similar trick a decade later with a different quartet of countries.

But in coming up with Growth Markets, I was not trying ambitiously to identify a new investment strategy. I, along with my colleagues, had simply concluded that it seemed an injustice, in economic terms, to still classify these four economies as 'emerging'. As already noted in the decade ahead their combined GDP will probably rise by around $16 trillion, beating the US increase almost fivefold and doubling the contribution to world growth of the US and the euro area combined, and they would soon be joined by others.

AFRICAN DREAMS

One popular idea has been to suggest that BRICs should in fact be BRICS, with the capital S for South Africa. Some argue it should be BRICA, with the A representing the African continent. As 2011 started, the S argument received a significant boost when it emerged that South Africa was being invited to the third annual meeting of the heads of state of the BRIC countries in Beijing. Some commentators believe South Africa is a natural member of BRICs, given its status as Africa's largest, and one of its wealthiest, economies. It also has an important position as a large commodity producer and has maintained long-term trade linkages with some of the BRIC economies, notably Brazil and India. And, of course, South Africa is already a member of the G20.

I will explore the BRIC political club in a later chapter, but as far as economic criteria are concerned it is difficult for me to think of South Africa as a genuine BRIC. It is even difficult to think of South Africa as a Growth Market. It has very little chance of becoming anything like the size of these economies.

Although South Africa is currently Africa's largest economy, it is only around $360 billion, some 0.5 per cent of global GDP. It is about half the size of Indonesia or Turkey. Moreover, and in contrast to most of the N-11 economies, South Africa does not have strong demographics. Its population is less than 50 million. This is considerably lower than all the N-11 except Korea (which would grow by another 20 million if the South ever unified with the North). South Africa's unemployment rate in mid-2011 is 24 per cent. It is hard to be big if you don't have many people and such a high proportion of them aren't working.

By suggesting that South Africa is not big enough to be a BRIC, I am not denying its regional importance. Indeed, the political argument for including South Africa in the BRIC might be that it is acting as a representative for the continent of Africa. (Whether other large African countries would see this as appropriate is another matter, but the rationale is understandable.) Africa as a continent is certainly large enough to be regarded as a BRIC: if you merely took the eleven largest African countries they would be of equivalent size to India or Russia, and their combined 2050 potential is on a par. If a continent could be thought of as a country, then perhaps we can think of BRICA.

Of course, as is the case for all the BRIC and N-11 economies, there is a huge difference between potential and reality. This is where GES analytics are so useful. In Africa's case, there needs to be considerable, and in some cases dramatic, improvement. In 2010 the average score for the African eleven economies was 3.8, a full 1 point below the average of the N-11 and BRIC economies. Some African countries have extremely low scores for reasons ranging from political instability to widespread corruption, weak or draconian governance, low educational standards and limited use of technology.

Unless these scores increase, then the potential for the continent will remain just that, 'potential'. Very few successful economies have such low scores. The two current largest of the BRIC economies, Brazil and China, score well above 5. While these scores are not high enough for either of them to reach their full potential, they are in a much better place than most African countries.

In principle, boosting their GES shouldn't be excessively difficult if African leaders were to adopt the best practices of the likes of Brazil and Korea. Formal inflation targeting would be an easy yet powerful strategy to pursue, as South Africa did some years ago. Giving such importance to low and stable inflation is a clear sign of transparency, something which is itself necessary in so many of these economies.

As far as the micro variables are concerned, the required steps here are even more important and perhaps trickier for some African countries – given their short independent histories and poor track record of governance. African leaders should eagerly target improvements in some of these variables in order to bring about the progress their populations crave and need: better education, improved health care to extend life expectancy, the use of mobiles and computers, and more stable and predictable forms of governance.

Demography is destiny, goes the saying, which if true makes Africa an even hotter prospect. In 2011 the United Nations published its revised estimates for the world's population in 2100. Asia will be home to 60 per cent of the world's population, as it is today. But Africa will swell. Between 1975 and 2000 it grew from 416 to 811 million. By 2025, it will reach 1.4 billion and by 2100 a remarkable 2.2 billion. In addition to Africa's well-known population giants Nigeria, Ethiopia and Congo, Tanzania is expected to grow to 138 million by 2050, Kenya from 47 to 59 million and Uganda may exceed 100 million.

The greatest challenges to Africa's growth may come from its growth environment scores. The average for the BRICs is 4.9, for the N-11, it is 4.7, but, as mentioned above, the very top eleven African countries average just 3.8 and for Africa as a whole it is a low 3.5. Morocco (5.5), Egypt (4.2) and South Africa (4.9) are towards the top, with countries like Zimbabwe (2.9) and Congo (1.7) at the bottom. Overall, the African countries lurk near the bottom of our 180-country GES ranking, and need to make a lot more progress across the board if they are to achieve their economic potential.

Nigeria, though, has shown what can be done. I recently bumped into the country's finance minister, Segun Aganga, who worked for Goldman Sachs' capital markets team until 2010. To my delight, he had with him Nigeria's growth environment scores. He told me that he was planning a marketing campaign around Nigeria's ambition to be twentieth on the world GES chart by 2020.

Nigeria is critical to Africa with around 20 per cent of the continent's population. Aganga's aspirations for the country make me really excited about where Africa's most populous economy can get to in the future. By 2100, Nigeria's population could well be bigger than that of the United States. It has a group of politicians who seem determined to weed out the terrible corruption which restricted its growth for so long. And, while its GES is the third lowest of the N-11 group, it has nearly doubled in the last thirteen years. A repeat of this over the next thirteen would have Nigeria well on its way to delivering its potential.

In this it will be aided by the technological leaps that are now possible. All over Africa, mobile wireless technology is enabling the rapid development of basic services like education and banking. If this continues and expands, countries like Nigeria may be able to grow at an unprecedented rate, skipping once necessary stages of development. This could be a very positive story in the years to come, and is yet another reminder that the world is about far more than stumbling growth in the United States and western Europe.

Even small improvements in the growth environment can have an enormous impact on a country's growth trajectory, and we estimated that Nigeria's efforts had helped lift its growth rate by 2 per cent. If it could raise its GES to best-in-class levels, it could raise this growth rate by another 4 per cent, a massive premium. Of course there are many variables at work here, but the important point is that the rise of Africa's middle class, when coupled with greater transparency and openness, and an improved environment for economic growth, could lead to one of the great economic stories in the coming years.

Remarkable events were unfolding in Egypt as I wrote this book. Within a little over two weeks President Mubarak was forced to stand down as the nation's leader. What appeared to start as a 'copycat' protest following unrest in Tunisia quickly turned into an uprising of the Egyptian people to reject decades of imposed governance and seemingly demanding a life of more opportunity, hope and perhaps democracy.

Quite where the nation will go is extremely unpredictable, and the answer is likely to be crucial on many fronts, especially given its historical role in the Middle East's security issues. Here is the Arab world's most populous country having a revolt, if not a revolution. No sign of American flags being burnt or anti-Western protest. On the contrary, lots of the most common signs from the protests are that Egyptian people, now having access to the internet and mobile phones, have suddenly seen what so many others have, and they want it for themselves. They are also agitated by high food prices, lack of employment, crumbling infrastructure, an over-bureaucratic state. It was the internet and mobile phones – social media – that gave them quick access to what was happening in Tunisia, to network and galvanize quickly around a common cause, or to find common cause through online discussions.

When the uprising occurred in Egypt in January 2011, I looked immediately to its growth environment. Egypt is an N-11 country, a nation of 80 million people. Its economy is only around $200 billion, so it is not one of the larger or wealthier N-11 nations. It has vast potential and what happens here is likely to be instrumental for much of North Africa and the Middle East. Egypt's GES of 4.22 ranked it eighth out of the N-11, just above Nigeria, Bangladesh and Pakistan. Over the previous decade, it had scarcely improved. Its macro scores, such as government debt and its fiscal position, were poor, as were micro scores such as use of technology and political stability. Watching the protestors on television, it was not hard to understand their frustration at years of economic stagnation.

As risk premia rose in financial markets all over the world, as people worried about these uprisings spreading throughout the Middle East and affecting the price of oil, my thought was that if these events end up improving Egypt's growth environment, and thus the well-being of its people, then it will have been worth it.

In Egypt, for example, the growth environment scores have been so low for so long that it did not surprise me when the people eventually said 'enough' and demanded new leadership. The spread of technology means they can easily see what has happened in China over the last few years – the quadrupling of wealth – and demand it for themselves. I tend to see most political and economic events through these scores. If a new regime can deliver more accountability of leadership and more opportunity for its people, then this could be an extremely positive development. Not just for Egypt, but for the whole region.

BE BIG OR BE WEALTHY?

I've often thought that many Western observers are 'scared' of the potential of the BRIC and N-11 countries, believing that their growth might be at the expense of their own countries' success. This is not the case. Not only is their potential just that – potential – but their success, if it occurs, is likely to be good for everyone else.

It's easy to forget that the BRIC countries have to raise their growth environment scores and productivity in order for their potential to be actually achieved. When they do so, I have sufficient faith in economics to believe that international trade is a win–win situation for us all, at least in the aggregate. It is the basic yet critical tenet of international trade that countries specialize in their net advantages, and through this, trade with each other. International trade benefits all. The emergence of the BRIC countries – and the N-11 – is boosting global trade in a dramatic way, and as a result helping the rest of the world.

It is equally important to remember that there is a difference between wealth and size. The US is the biggest economy in the world today and has been for decades. But in terms of wealth per capita, it is not the richest. Bermuda, Luxembourg, Switzerland, most of the Scandinavian countries are all considerably richer than the US. The US becoming bigger doesn't threaten those countries' wealth. In fact, because of international trade, as the US has grown it has helped those countries to become wealthier. The same is true as a result of the emergence of China, the rest of the BRICs and the broader world.

Looking at the world's most populous nations in terms of future wealth, rather than overall GDP, not many of today's big developing countries are likely to become anywhere near as wealthy as those in the so-called developed world. Russia, from the BRICs, ironically, does have the chance to be among the more wealthy nations, possibly becoming as wealthy as the larger European economies. Of the Next Eleven, Korea and Mexico could conceivably rise to be among the top ten wealthiest countries in the world if they achieve their potential.

None of the others is likely to come close to the wealth enjoyed by today's most wealthy nations, although a number could attain levels of GDP per capita similar to those achieved in some of them. China will probably become an exceptionally large economy by 2050, not far off double that of the US, but its wealth is likely to be just half. India will only represent a quarter of the wealth of the US, at best.

THE RISE OF GROWTH MARKETS

A simple glance at the performance of Germany in recent years is a powerful example of the positive forces that can be unleashed by the rise of the Growth Markets. As a large exporting nation, the growth of world trade is critical to Germany's prosperity, and its exports to some of the BRIC countries are rising dramatically. German exports to the four BRICs have already become bigger than its exports to France; at the time of writing, China looks set to become its third largest market within a few months. If sustained close to this pace for another couple of years, it would lead to German trade with China being bigger than German trade with France, a quite remarkable development given those two nations' close proximity and modern history.

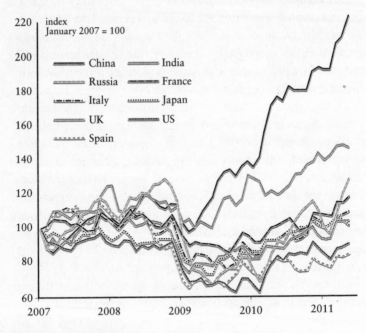

German Exports since 2007

Source: Haver Analytics, Goldman Sachs calculations

Many people still argue that these nations are not the growth engines that I claim. They say I could have used the same arguments at any time in history, and their emergence as major successful economies still hasn't happened. But, as I have already explained, we did test the BRIC models back to fifty years ago – and we saw that many Asian economies ended up bigger than the model would have predicted.

A major goal for all the BRIC and N-11 countries must be to undertake policies to raise their GES to Korea-like levels. If they do, the dramatic 2050 scenarios are going to be achieved. Korea has GES which are better than all the G7 countries except Canada. If the rest of the 'growth economies' achieved these levels then I am sure we would all be better off.

In addition to the critical policies each BRIC nation will individually need to introduce, there is one common variable that suggests the next fifty years are to be more supportive for their economies than the last: technology. New developments in communications mean the world is going through another dramatic phase of globalization, where national economic borders are being eroded and countries can easily participate in global business and markets. This is especially new for China and Russia, who entered the world economy as recently as the 1980s. China's and Russia's self-imposed post-war exile in terms of Western ideas and economic policies is over, and 1.3 billion Chinese and 140 million Russians have joined the rest of us in the consumer society.

Witness Manchester United's reported 70 million Chinese website members, the thriving McDonald's restaurants and fashionable clothing stores in the major cities of both countries and the huge expansion of luxury goods sales both in the BRIC countries and to BRIC tourists in the West.

China's appearance on the international stage has been highly important for others. Take India: some critical domestic factors offer India a brighter future, but China's remarkable success has made many Indian policymakers sit up and engage more widely with the world economy.

China's success has similarly stimulated some of the N-11 economies: hence why I am so optimistic about the world's future. The growth economies are raising their potential and also ours. Proactive engagement in international trade has been a hugely positive force for each of the BRIC nations in the past decade, as has the adoption of best economic practice from Western macro policies (perhaps more questionable since the global credit crisis). Just look at the way inflation targeting has transformed Brazil.

With so many people now rising up the economic ranks, from poverty towards middle-class incomes and lifestyles, the planet's resources are coming under unprecedented strain, and it is to this aspect of global growth that I shall turn next.

5

Are There Enough Resources?

It has been a natural fear for centuries that the more of us occupy the planet the fewer resources there will be to go round. The eighteenth-century English scholar Thomas Malthus painted the most famous and grimmest picture in his *Essay on the Principle of Population*, in which he described a tension between population and our means of subsistence. Whenever there are too many people, he wrote, what followed was 'misery and vice' in the form of epidemics, famines, war and extreme poverty, until the balance between people and their means of subsistence was restored.

There are many today who look at the rise of the BRICs and see the realization of Malthus's fears. So many new people with so many demands for food, energy and consumer goods must inevitably upend the global supply of resources. If there is a single reason the BRIC dream I outlined for 2050 won't materialize, goes their argument, it is the lack of resources to satisfy this hungry new world. Others express the connected, but different, fear that such rapid growth will exacerbate climate change and lead to such erosion of the world's ecology that it will force us to slow down. Advocates of these views point to the persistent rise in many commodity prices since 2000 reflecting intensifying demand for limited supply as evidence to support their thinking.

There is no doubt that resources will be crucial to the growth of the BRICs, and their relations with the rest of the world, which is why in 2004 my colleagues analysed the energy markets, oil in particular, in the context of our predictions for the BRICs in 2050. They found that if the BRICs grew at the pace we thought they could between 2005 and 2050, then a major imbalance would develop between the supply and demand of energy resources.[1]

I also wrote a paper in 2004 showing that China's role in driving demand would be critical.[2] As by far the biggest of the BRICs, China's need for resources would continue to drive up the price of oil and many other commodities unless it fell significantly short of expectations in terms of economic growth, or found some way round using traditional energy supplies, whether through new technology, increased efficiency or alternative sources. At the time of this research, there was no hint that Chinese policymakers were looking for such alternatives. By 2010, their view had changed and with it my own view of the future for commodity prices. I am not sure that the long-term bull market in commodity prices is as powerful as I thought it was in 2005. In fact, I side more than ever with the optimists, who argue that the reason Malthus's worst fears never came to pass and will not in the foreseeable future, is technology.

At key moments in human history, man has found solutions to his most acute problems. An oft-quoted example of this was the great horse-manure crisis which afflicted America's cities in the late nineteenth century. In New York in 1900 the population of 100,000 horses reportedly produced

2.5 million pounds of manure every day. Streets were apparently covered with the stuff and the air was thick with flies. *The Times* speculated that by the middle of the twentieth century, London would be buried under nine feet of horse droppings. The future of cities was at stake. What saved them was the arrival of motorized transport. The entire manure problem vanished at a stroke, courtesy of men like Henry Ford.

I'm not suggesting that feeding the BRICs' appetite for resources will be easy. Nor do I wish to trivialize the challenge it presents. But I do have faith that scientific innovation, wise government policy and the markets can provide solutions which will help us avoid the doomsayers' scenarios. As nations become richer and individuals prosper, it stimulates business to search for new ideas and creative technologies that will drive the future.

Economists, however, make a mistake when they focus on the supply-and-demand issues of today without looking either back at historical patterns or out into the future. In 2001, when I dreamt up the BRIC acronym, the popular view was that commodities were a poor business and that prices only ever went down. Most energy- or commodity-industry executives I spoke to were very cautious about making new investments. The CEOs made constant reference to the 1970s and early 1980s and worked on the assumption that underlying crude-oil prices would be around $35 per barrel. This was the basis for all their investments. Yet between the end of 2001 and the beginning of 2011, the IMF's global commodity index rose fourfold.

In January 2005 I participated in the annual meeting of the top executives of a leading European-based energy company. After making my presentation about the BRICs dream and the world economy, I was invited, with two other guests, to debate our views with the company's CEO. The price per barrel of oil at the time was around $42, and the CEO asked me how confident I was this would not drop to $28 within a year. His anxiety was typical among energy and commodity executives. They worried that by responding to rising prices by increasing investment, they would be caught out when supplies increased and prices fell. Most would much rather be conservative, pay higher dividends and buy back shares rather than invest in the long-term and expensive expansion of their capacity. This logical response to the volatility of commodity prices might, ironically, have been partly what kept them so high.

But trying to apply economic logic to commodity prices can easily threaten your sanity, as I discovered when I was still studying.

In my judgement, it is important to distinguish between real trends and noise. While it is always difficult, the ability to do so is what ultimately marks out good analysts from bad. The lazy consensus back in the early 1980s among many economists was that the future would exactly resemble the immediate past and present. They misunderstood the way supply and demand respond to oil prices. In the short term, not much changes. OPEC can increase or decrease production at short notice, but developing new fields and building the infrastructure to ship and refine large supplies of oil takes time. Over longer periods, however, countries, companies and individuals can dramatically affect the supply and demand of energy, by developing new sources and changing consumption habits. Oil prices are affected, of course, by supply and demand, but they also themselves affect supply and demand. The more oil costs, the fewer people want to heat their houses with it, or use it to get to work. It takes time for such changes to work through a society, but if high prices persist, they do. Or, in economic terms, the long-term elasticity of supply and demand is higher than the short-term elasticity, and possibly higher than many economists believe. I have no reason to doubt that this experience will play out again. When I look at China in 2011, its supply-and-demand response to higher energy prices reminds me of some things that happened with global energy supply and demand back in the early 1980s, just after I'd finished my PhD on the topic.

Taking this view involved re-examining the forecasts my colleagues made in 2004. Given rising demand in China and India, and to a lesser extent Russia and Brazil, they envisaged a scenario between 2005 and 2020 in which world oil demand would grow on average by 2 per cent a year, a significant rise from 1.4 per cent a year over the previous two decades. Similar projections could doubtless have been made for other commodities. Beyond 2020, however, they forecast demand flattening out. Their reasoning was based on economic theory and empirical evidence from Korea and Japan which suggests that as a nation's GDP per capita rises from very low levels its energy usage intensifies, hitting its peak when GDP per capita reaches around $6,000 (at 2003 values). As per capita wealth increases, incremental increase in energy use then tapers off, eventually converging with the rates we see in more advanced societies.

Economists explain this by saying that the intensity of energy usage follows an S curve, starting slow, speeding up and then flattening out during a more mature stage when energy efficiency improves. Economists also utilize a concept known as purchasing power parity, or PPP. The idea of PPP is that identical goods should cost the same in different markets, and the exchange rate should reflect that. The $6,000 figure given by my colleagues was based on the purchasing power of the US dollar in 2003, for example. Today it would be about $7,500. In layman's terms, under PPP the price of a cup of coffee in New York converted into euros should buy you a cup of coffee in Paris. Chinese GDP per capita in 2011 in PPP terms is now around $7,500 while India's is still somewhat behind, at around $3,300.

One interpretation of why this S curve exists is that as people first 'discover' wealth, they spend freely to acquire new and exciting luxuries. In developing countries one of the very first things people buy as they move up the economic ladder is a car, immediately intensifying their energy demands. I have already described the contrasting journeys from Beijing airport to the city centre in 2011 and twenty years ago. In the early 1990s, the biggest obstacle was the hundreds of cyclists and their carts piled high with vegetables and fruit coming into town from the countryside. Today, the journey comes with the same frustrations experienced in most major cities in the West: car traffic and congestion. The same pattern is emerging in many other Chinese cities and is set to occur in many urban areas of India. Only as people become richer and more used to their wealth do they start to prize energy efficiency over consumption.

We clearly have some way to go before the BRICs reach the top of the S curve and moderate their energy use according to this model. China is getting close but India remains a long way off. Until then, the energy and commodity markets will face severe difficulties in matching supply to demand. There will be times when it feels as if the world has insufficient resources, just as it might seem that rising commodity prices are about to unleash a period of high inflation and economic volatility, as they did in the 1970s. We are already seeing new alliances emerging between the commodity-hungry BRICs and commodity producers all over the world. These alliances are bringing commodity-rich Brazil and Russia closer to China and India. Commodity producers across Africa are being courted by China. This may explain why South Africa has been welcomed so readily into the BRIC political club. A significant commodity producer itself, it may also be seen by China and India as a beachhead into Africa.

But I also believe that there will be other factors which could significantly alter the upward trend of resource and commodity prices and consumption. For example, China and India might not grow as quickly as I predict. A stronger world growth trend over the next twenty years is highly dependent on China and India. If either or both, especially China, fail to grow close to projected rates or find much more efficient forms of energy consumption earlier than is typical for countries at their stage of development, then the projections for global energy demand during the period 2005–20 might need to be revised downwards. I have heard it argued that the pressure on resource prices and availability will persist regardless of what happens in China and India. I find this difficult to believe. What happens with regard to their demand for both energy and resources overall is going to be dominant for the commodity supply industry, at least on the demand side of the equation. The future of the world economy in the coming decades hinges on growth in the BRIC countries and the United States. Growth may ease in Japan and Europe, even China and Russia as their populations age. But along with Brazil, India and the United States, which are likely to see ever-growing populations, they will have a decisive impact on the growth of the world economy – and this will be critical for the demand for world energy. All of this seems to have extremely powerful implications for world energy prices and raises fears about the availability of resources, but it might not be quite so straightforward. A lot will depend on the decisions of producing companies as well as energy users as prices adjust.

Remember those energy company executives in 2005 who thought that the equilibrium oil price was around $35, and worried that prices might not be sustained much above that level. As a result, many were highly reluctant to invest. By 2011, with $35 a distant memory, and prices far above that for years, many had changed their minds. They now think we have reached a new higher equilibrium, and they could be right, but just as I found when I was studying for my PhD all those years ago, that equally might not be true – at least not for long. With oil prices as high as they are today, energy companies may be encouraged to invest in additional production, and consumers may seek alternatives to expensive oil. If this happens, any strong perception that today's prices represent a new equilibrium might quickly be proved illusory.

Another significant change since 2004, and one that has latterly increased in momentum, is the attitude in China and India towards developing alternative sources of energy. The industrialization and urbanization of China are undoubtedly the main drivers of the current super-cycle in commodity prices and production. But no one enjoys paying high prices for energy and commodities, so in addition to developing its supplies of traditional fossil fuels, China has also launched a vigorous programme of investment and support for renewable energy. Western critics may point at China's polluted cities and rivers and call the country's growth unsustainable, but China's leaders see exactly the same problems, feel them even more acutely than these distant critics, and are busily seeking solutions.

By 2020, China plans to have reduced its carbon intensity by between 40 per cent and 45 per cent compared with 2005 levels.[3] Writing in the *Financial Times* in November 2009,[4] Sir Gordon Conway, co-chair of the China Council for International Cooperation on Environment and Development (CCICED), described China's plan for a low-carbon economy. 'The Chinese leaders are moved by a sense of urgency,' he wrote. 'Following the traditional economic model is not an option: resource, social and environmental constraints make it impossible. They are also aware of the danger that rapid growth will lock China into industrial and urban structures that will become a liability in a low-carbon world.' As a result, the Chinese leadership had asked the CCICED to draw up three scenarios. Under the first, China continues down its current path of energy consumption, and produces nearly 13 billion tonnes of carbon dioxide by 2050, nearly twice what it produces today (already more than the US and Canada combined). The second scenario would limit emissions to 9 billion tonnes by 2050. The third would let emissions peak in 2025 and then fall to 5 billion by 2050, equivalent to what the United States emits today.

The key to cutting emissions, wrote Conway, was 'decoupling growth from greenhouse gas emissions'. This would mean reducing energy consumption per unit of GDP by 75–85 per cent by 2050, through a comprehensive efficiency scheme, involving everything from low-carbon cities and transport systems to revamped factories. Fossil fuels would be used more efficiently, use of renewables and nuclear energy would expand, and carbon-heavy emissions would be captured before they polluted the environment. Not only do the Chinese see this plan as a means to cleaner air and water, and less dependence on fluctuating fossil fuel prices, but they also see it as a way for China to develop a competitive advantage in a low-carbon world. The ambition and detail of this policy far outstrip anything we have seen from the United States.

Applying the impact of China's low-carbon measures to predictions for China's oil consumption in 2050 is fascinating. If China were to succeed in supplying 50 per cent of its new energy needs with renewable resources by 2030, and 100 per cent by 2050, as the CCICED reports it hopes to, then this would have a dramatic effect on our projections for global oil demand. In 2004 we predicted that the world would be using 75.2 million barrels of oil per day by 2050. Assuming the Chinese do what they intend, then that estimate is 20 per cent too high. The world in 2050 will be using just 60 million barrels of oil per day. If India were to commit to similar targets, that would slash a further 20 million barrels per day from our 2004 projection for oil consumption by 2050.

This Chinese initiative strikes me as extremely exciting and should prove quite a stimulant for the supply of energy from sustainable sources. It surprises me that professional commodity market participants are not more focused on China's plans. I certainly keep an eye on them, and try to track the government's progress. The *China Daily* now publishes a weekly European edition and in May 2011 devoted five full pages, including the front page, to the topic of electric cars. The newspaper discussed the likely future demand for automobiles in China, citing the Ministry of Industry and Information Technology's intention that there should be more than 200 million registered vehicles by 2020, up from 70 million in 2011. The government has announced its commitment to spending approximately $15 billion over the next decade to boost electric car development. This follows a 2010 commitment to boosting the number of electric-powered vehicles by 20 million by 2020. China's influential National Development and Reform Commission has said that it is looking to subsidize the cost of at least 4 million electric-powered vehicles and that the government is already trialling their use in the country's main cities, including Beijing and Shanghai.

The two main problems with electric cars are the high cost of batteries and their limited range. The Chinese recognize this and are doing all they can to support the growing battery industry. As most driving in China is done in cities, with distances of less than sixty kilometres per day, they see electric cars as being potentially as viable and easy to use as iPhones. The whole world stands to benefit from China's concerted investment and focus in this field. (My personal investment portfolio includes shares in a small Swedish Solar Power Company and the stories that I hear about Chinese interest in it are remarkable.)

It will not be straightforward for China to achieve its ambitious goals for energy conservation and improved efficiency. Announcing plans to boost the use of alternative energies, electric cars and the like is easy. Actually to achieve them in a country in which about 50 per cent of its population still lives in rural communities – of whom at least a third will move into cities in the next twenty years – is difficult. That being said, with strong central leadership, China is better placed to implement such tough goals than others.

So we have a complex world evolving in the commodity

markets, with strong price pressures influencing many aspects of the world economy. But just as in the 1980s there was a response to the rising prices, it seems likely that the same will occur this time. Much will depend on how countries can coordinate and cooperate to respond to these immense challenges.

6

Consumption

When I visit China today I wonder whether this was how the California gold rush felt in the middle of the nineteenth century. There are lots of unknowns, lots of uncertainty, plenty of risk and occasionally even physical danger. The rules of the game are not entirely clear. But everyone can see the potential and everyone wants in. The discovery of gold in California persuaded many nineteenth-century Americans to pack up and heed the popular calls to 'Go west, young man'. In the early twenty-first century, those in search of opportunity must look east to Asia and south to Latin America and Africa.

The rising levels of consumption in the BRIC countries are a compelling sign of how quickly these economies are changing. Consumption and foreign direct investment are the components of GDP which I follow most closely. They tell me how a country is maturing, how much wealthier its people are becoming, what they are choosing to buy, and to what extent their economy is opening up to the world. Fast-growing domestic consumption in a developing economy is a good predictor of stability and long-term growth. Increased foreign direct investment indicates how credible the world finds that growth.

There is already plenty of anecdotal evidence of rising BRIC consumption. In summer 2009 my wife and I visited Engelberg, a lovely Swiss resort that could have been the setting for *The Sound of Music*. Before we left, we had heard that many Bollywood films were shot there, and that as a result it had become a popular destination for Indian tourists. Sure enough, we found Indians on every ski lift going up to take in the mountain views. At the foot of the main lift, there was even a van selling Indian food. Two years later, in spring 2011, we returned to Switzerland, to Les Diablerets, before going on to Lausanne for the Financial Times Luxury Goods Conference. The town was quiet, in between the busy winter skiing and summer hiking seasons. We took a walk to a beautiful spot called Col du Pillon from where you could take a lift up to 3,000 metres, and see the highest Swiss mountains. It was 77 francs for each of us to go up and down. At the then exchange rate, the whole excursion for both of us would cost £113.66. We debated whether it was worth the money, and decided to go up. Needless to say, it was cold and cloudy at the top and hard to see much, and we came straight back down. But what struck me about the experience is that at the lower entrance to the lift and at the expensive café at the top, Indians surrounded us. Just after I bought tickets for my wife and myself an Indian gentleman handed over 600 Swiss francs in cash for himself and several friends. At the summit café were maybe a hundred more Indians, spending money and enjoying themselves even though all they could see were clouds.

On our way back down, we saw an advertisement on the lift wall for HSBC Private Bank. It consisted of a picture of a major Chinese city, perhaps Hong Kong or Shanghai, and the claim that HSBC was the best 'emerging market bank' in the world. The story of the increasingly wealthy BRIC consumer had followed me all the way up a Swiss mountain. If, as I suspect, India does see its wealth rise thirtyfold in the next forty years, there won't just be Swiss cafés and Indian food trucks in these mountains, but proper, top-notch Indian restaurants alongside the traditional European ones. You will be able to ski in or hike up and choose between Rösti and a curry.

In London, the top end of the property market is almost entirely driven by non-British buyers, many from the BRICs. Apartments in South Beach in Miami are now being snapped up by Brazilians. Wealthy Chinese travel and shop in Paris and Tokyo en masse. Russian tourists have been a fixture in the most fashionable European resorts for years now, mooring their yachts in St-Tropez or skiing in Courchevel, where they flock for the New Year and Russian Orthodox Christmas in the first two weeks of January. They are also expanding their property buying, from London, ski resorts and the south of France to Greece and Turkey. Europe – and potentially the US – stands to gain from the eventual arrival of millions of BRIC tourists.

The economic evidence of rapid growth in BRIC consumption is at least as compelling as the anecdotes. At the end of 2010 consumption in the BRIC countries came to about $5 trillion. In the United States it was $10.5 trillion, in the European Union $9.5 trillion and in Japan around $3 trillion. Significantly, though, the growth rates in these different markets were dramatically different. In 2000, BRIC consumption was just $1.4 trillion, so the increase to $5 trillion represents an increase of 250 per cent over just ten years. If this pattern persists, at least up to the end of this decade, the

BRIC consumer markets could be worth $12 trillion or more, easily rivalling the United States.

In a paper written with my colleague Anna Stupnytska in December 2010, she and I looked at alternative scenarios for BRIC consumption between 2010 and 2025.[1] In the first scenario, we assumed a 'status quo' in which the average share of consumption as a percentage of overall GDP remained the same as it was over the previous decade. Here we found consumption in the BRICs would rise fourfold by 2025, to more than $16 trillion, bigger than the market in the United States. China would be responsible for around half this total, with a real value of close to $10 trillion. India would become the clear second largest, rising to between $3 and $4 trillion.

In an alternative, more optimistic scenario, we assumed that as these economies became more dependent on domestic consumption, and less on exports, for GDP growth, consumer share of GDP would rise. In China, for example, we estimated that the consumer share of GDP would rise to 43 per cent by 2015 and 55 per cent by 2025. In this scenario, the real value of BRIC consumption would rise fivefold, and China alone could exceed the US in real terms by 2025. In nominal terms, the Chinese consumer could become worth $20 trillion. The aggregate value of the BRIC consumer would rise each year on average by $2 trillion, taking it to $35 trillion by 2025. Anna and I applied these macro-economic assumptions for the BRIC consumer to some key specific consumer markets and showed that, if they are correct, the BRIC markets will dominate certain industries, notably cars, luxury goods, travel and tourism.

Both in theory and based on experience, this second scenario is more likely. As happens with energy demand (see

Chapter 5), in developing countries we tend to find that rising wealth creates an S-shaped pattern for consumer durable expenditures. Each of the UK, US, Japan and Korea have followed these patterns. It takes a while for people to recognize their own wealth and for companies to deliver products they can buy. But once consumer habits are formed and nourished, progress is swift. Applying this model to the BRIC countries, especially China, results in a prediction of extraordinary growth in demand for consumer products. China, by this measure, is around where South Korea was in 1980, on the brink of a significant consumer take-off.

Applying this approach to the motor industry offers an even richer sense of the scale of the consumer opportunity. By 2050 the Chinese could own twice as many cars as Americans, and India nearly three times as many. Brazilians may own more cars than the combined total in Germany and Japan, and Russians could own more than Germans. Goldman Sachs' equity analysts predict that in the years up to 2020, most of the growth in the global auto industry will come from the BRICs. By 2020 they reckon that 70 per cent of all cars, around 50 million, will be bought in BRIC countries. China could account for half of these. It is not hard to see why the world's leading motor manufacturers are so focused on these markets. The strong branded German companies – Daimler, BMW, Audi – are already seeing dramatic growth. A quality German car has become an important status symbol for consumers who would think twice about paying so much for many other things. General Motors, a company that used to symbolize the strength of the United States, has arguably become a company dominated by Chinese business. Suzuki, the Japanese company, is making major inroads into India.

When I talk to auto executives I find that their concerns about the global economy have changed in the past decade. In the 1990s, they would want to know my views on exchange rates, and whether sharp moves in the dollar, yen or European currencies might hurt their profitability. In recent years they have wanted to hear my projections for the BRICs, and to better understand the risks and opportunities in these markets. For the first time in my career, more of them seem motivated by hope than by fear, and many have smiles on their faces.

Take China: many multinationals first went to the country to take advantage of its cheap labour. They saw a chance to improve profitability through lower costs. But what first brought them into this market is not what is keeping them there. As wages rise, the labour cost advantage of manufacturing in China is eroding. These days, the greatest opportunity is for those companies with the strongest brands. A huge and expanding population now desires and can afford their products. The reality of this came home to me when talking to a colleague in Frankfurt, who wanted to surprise his wife for her birthday by buying her a BMW. When he called his local dealership, he was told he would have to wait six months for the model he wanted, as there was such high demand for it in China. A BMW executive confirmed that this is often the case these days. Not even Germans can buy the BMWs they want when they want them any more.

Chinese companies have quickly caught on to the importance of brand over cost as a competitive advantage. Every year WPP, a world leader in advertising, conducts a survey to find the world's top 100 most valuable brands. Its 2011 listing includes several Chinese companies: China Mobile ranked 9, ICBC, China's biggest bank, at 11, and Baidu, the search engine, at 29. By 2020 there are bound to be more, perhaps as many as there are American names.

No industry has benefited more from the BRICs' rise so far than luxury goods. A few years ago I invested in a very small luxury Chinese Jewellery Company set up by French and Chinese founders. It seemed to me a good bet on the rising prosperity of the Chinese consumer. Chinese consumers will be attracted to many strong global luxury brands, but I also suspected that if there are genuine luxury brands of their own, then they would be likely to prosper too. The company, Qeelin, has its most successful outlets in the most fashionable shopping malls in Hong Kong and is expanding in Beijing and Shanghai. The Hong Kong store's biggest customers are generally mainland Chinese tourists. At the time of writing in mid-2011, a number of bigger luxury goods companies are trying to purchase the company.

My work on exchange rates was rarely of much interest to luxury goods firms, but these days they frequently ask for my thoughts about the world and invite me to attend their conferences. At the 2011 Financial Times Luxury Goods Conference in Lausanne I debated the state of the global economy with the newspaper's chief economics editor, Martin Wolf, and my ex-colleague Gavyn Davies. We were the opening act ahead of various panels featuring many leading luxury goods brands. It was no surprise to hear most of these companies expressing their great ambitions in the BRIC countries.

One of Goldman Sachs' luxury goods analysts, Will Hutchings, briefed me for the event. In China, he told me, 1 in every 1,400 people is a US-dollar millionaire, and there are nearly 200,000 of them in Beijing alone. In the next fifteen years, an additional 500 million-plus people globally will become luxury goods purchasers. About 200 million of them alone will be Chinese. India will be the next biggest growing purchaser, and both Brazil and Russia will be significant. For many Western companies, maintaining or adjusting their brand to attract these new consumers will be vital, indeed possibly transformational. And it won't just be about investing more in stores in the major BRIC cities. In fact, foreign 'luxury' cities such as Paris, Miami, New York and London will benefit. According to Will, 55 per cent of Brazilian luxury good purchases are made outside Brazil, mainly in Miami, which is to Brazilian luxury shoppers as Hong Kong is to the Chinese. Westerners worried about missing out on the changing pattern of world growth need to be a bit more open-minded. There are many opportunities for Western companies to benefit, especially those with strong brands.

The art market is similarly being transformed by the BRICs. Ed Dolman, the ex-chairman of Christie's auctioneers, tells me of the shifting demands on his travel schedule, with ever more flights to Beijing, Shanghai, Moscow. In the coming years, I am sure Mumbai will join the list along with other Chinese and Indian cities, as well as Rio and São Paulo. I wouldn't be surprised to see new auction houses emerging within the BRIC countries.

Many financial market professionals who examine the BRIC story tend to focus on commodities. While it is true that the BRIC countries have a thirst for commodities, a much more significant story lies in how they are starting to behave as consumers. For most of my career, the dominant group in the world economy was US consumers. Everything seemed to revolve around the buying habits of Americans. As the BRIC countries grow, their consumers will become the most important in the world. Chinese people already buy more cars than any other nation, 13.5 million in 2010 to America's 11.6 million. It could soon be the biggest market for luxury goods. The Chinese government has made increasing domestic consumption one of its economic priorities in the five-year plan laid out in 2011.

Since 2001, the value of BRIC GDP has more than trebled from around $3 trillion to around $12 trillion. Although by the end of 2010 the US-dollar value of the BRIC consumer, $5 trillion, was still less than half that of the US, the gap will soon narrow. By 2020, the value of the combined level of retail sales in the BRIC countries might be bigger than in the US.

It is quite simply the story of our generation. It is a reflection of their dramatically rising wealth, and reflects the desire of their near 3 billion people for the same consumer goods that we all desire in the West.

The key statistic for tracking the growth in demand for consumer goods is GDP per capita, which is rising sharply across the BRICs, but especially in China. Rising GDP concentrated in a few hands does not propel a mass consumer market. But when lots of people are getting richer quicker it creates a market for millions of new cars, refrigerators, air-conditioning systems, electrical and electronic goods, hi-tech gadgets, holidays, luxury goods, financial advice ... the list never ends. In all of the BRICs, but in China and India especially, the potential increase in wealth by 2050 is fantastic. For producers of consumer products, the potential markets are spectacular.

Western companies understand this. They see it first hand on their income statements. If you spend any time at BMW's headquarters in Munich, you end up thinking that what's going on in China is more important than what's going on in Germany. Talk to executives at Louis Vuitton or Tesco, and you will soon understand the structural theme driving these companies. Huge new consumer markets are opening up at a rate not seen since the United States emerged as the largest single consumer market in the late nineteenth and early twentieth centuries.

For the major Western economies, the rise of the BRIC consumer should be great news. It means they can stop seeing these countries as low-cost threats, and start to enjoy the profits to be had from selling to BRIC consumers. For multinationals, the BRICs are upending their pre-existing business models, for the better.

In mid-2011 Kentucky Fried Chicken already had 3,700 restaurants in China, three times more than its rival McDonald's, which is much larger in the United States. It has thrived by allowing its Chinese managers the flexibility to adapt their menus to Chinese tastes, leading to fewer chicken wings and more local dishes. Nestlé, Procter & Gamble and Unilever have thriving businesses in China, and in July 2011, Nestlé revealed it is trying to buy Hsu Fu Chi, one of China's biggest makers of sweets and baked goods, which was valued at the time on the Singapore stock exchange at $2.6 billion. Every week, it seems, I hear another staggering story of changes in Chinese consumption. Japan's English language *Nikkei Weekly* reported in mid-2011 that the average Chinese woman passing through Tokyo's Narita airport spends $1,000 on cosmetics.

My own employer, Goldman Sachs, stands to benefit if the BRICs' capital markets develop along with the rest of their economies. Even if policymakers choose to stick with conservative models for financial market development, the potential for significant growth is large. If they choose to pursue 'market based' systems akin to that of the US, then the potential is enormous. In such circumstances, global financial institutions, including investment banks, are likely to find great attraction to these markets.

Goldman Sachs has, of course, developed a strategy based around expansion in the BRIC countries. In less than twenty years Goldman could be employing more people in asset management or advisory businesses in Asia than in the rest of the world combined. Either that or many of those employed in those specialities elsewhere in the world will be providing these services to Asian-based clients. Similarly, in Europe, the opportunities that arise in Russia are likely to be quite substantial.

Another important indicator of BRIC consumption is the pace of urbanization. My experience tells me that there is something about urbanization which accelerates growth and increases prosperity. It could be as simple as 'keeping up with the Joneses'. People who live in close proximity to others want what they have or more and this stimulates economic competition, which leads to faster growth. Proximity also speeds up the transfer of knowledge. Ideas can be quickly shared and improved upon.

In India, as in China, new cities are sprouting up all over the country. When I worked in foreign exchange we used to say that you should not have a view on a country's currency unless you knew the name of its finance minister. These days I tell people that you shouldn't have a view on China unless you know the names of its most important cities. I once tried learning the name of every Chinese city with more than 5 million people, but quickly had to give up. When the G20 met in Nanjing in 2010, I confess I'd never heard of the place. Yet Jiangsu, its surrounding province, is bigger than Germany. (Incidentally, one of the only European countries to offer direct flights to Nanjing is Germany, an indication of the strengthening ties between them.)

In India at least fifty cities have a population of more than a million people. So many people living close together, inching up the economic ladder and wanting what so many others have, is a dream for consumer companies. It's no surprise that executives from fashion, style and leisure industries are swarming through these markets to understand their potential.

In 2005 I served briefly on the board of Manchester United Football Club. The evolution of English and world football shows the astonishing impact of the BRICs. It used to be that English clubs coveted Brazilian players; now it's Russian, Asian and Middle Eastern billionaires who scramble to own English clubs.

In 2008 I flew to Mumbai during a European Champions League game in which Manchester United were playing Barcelona. When I arrived at the airport it was half time. I told my driver to drive as fast as he could to my hotel, and he got there with ten minutes of the game left to play. I asked the receptionist and the porter to take me up to my room as quickly as possible. Once we got there they stood behind me watching the game, as gripped as I was. At the end of the match – we beat them, for once – I sent a message to the then chief executive of the club, David Gill, saying: 'Next marketing trick: India.' Who knows, maybe in another ten years United will be fielding football teams in China and India.

*

Shortly before I attended that *FT* conference in Switzerland, the Chinese Academy of Social Sciences (CASS) forecast that the US-dollar value of Chinese consumption will almost double by 2015 to around $4 trillion. A $2 trillion increase in five years, or $400 billion per year, is the kind of expansion not even the pre-credit-crisis binge US consumer could manage. Post-crisis, it would take the US somewhere between ten and twenty years to achieve this. To my surprise, when I mentioned the CASS forecast in Lausanne during our panel, the others didn't seem to think it was such a big deal.

This refusal to accept the importance of what is happening among BRIC consumers is, oddly, not unusual. Many Western commentators struggle to understand and interpret it, and fall back on fear and bias. It is part of a broader pattern of stubborn denial in the face of overwhelming evidence. Some of it is just a simple fear of the unknown. Despite the smiles I find on the faces of executives at multinationals about the rise of the BRICs, it is inevitable that such a major shift in economic power will make people uncomfortable.

Occasionally I hear politicians or investors trying to argue that China is not yet ready to be the world's biggest economy. That it cannot make the leap from an export-driven economy to one driven by domestic consumption. That it is not ready to assume the global, political role commensurate with its economic muscle. On the first point, I disagree. The assumption that China cannot continue to grow and evolve as an economy seems based on the prejudice that they will forever be old-fashioned Soviet-style communists. I believe that by 2013, China could conceivably run a trade deficit, a sign that its dependence on exports is waning. On the second point, the evidence is conflicting.

There will clearly be complications as BRIC consumers

soak up ever more consumer goods. My colleague who had to wait six months for a BMW suffered no great hardship. But what if his problem became more widespread and endemic, if increased BRIC demand led to higher prices and forced consumer goods beyond the economic reach of many Western consumers? It is easy to see resentments forming and protectionist attitudes taking hold.

Of course, smart, forward-looking companies will be adapting their brands and cost structures to suit the tastes and aspirations in the new markets, which will be different from the traditional ones. The need for mental as well as procedural adjustment in the so-called industrialized economies will be substantial. Germany in some ways is becoming a role model. Since 2007 German exports to China and India have risen dramatically. As I've said, at the current pace, by 2012 German trade with China may outstrip German trade with France. How remarkable is that? In early 2011 Bosch, the German specialist machine parts maker, announced it was boosting employment by more than 30,000 people mainly because of their growth in exports to the emerging world. By the spring of 2011 German employment overall had surpassed its pre-credit-crisis levels, testimony to German manufacturers' export powers.

I believe that people in developed economies can follow the German model and reap benefits, such as more jobs, from exporting more to the BRICs. But Japan, other European nations and the United States will all have to adjust to profit from the powerful changes underway.

I find myself thinking that BRIC growth and world growth can go hand in hand. Higher growth in one part of the world does not require lower growth in another. Over the past thirty years world GDP growth has averaged around 3.7 per cent per year. Between 2000 and 2010 it rose to 4 per cent despite the collapse in 2009. As I write in mid-2011, two and a half years after the global credit crisis, the consensus forecast for world GDP growth in 2011 is 3.9 per cent and in 2012 4.1 per cent. The BRICs, in my opinion, are driving this higher growth rate around the world – both directly and indirectly.

Many of the Western-based branded goods companies I have discussed are showing very strong earnings growth. The power of the BRIC story can also be seen in the pattern of global consumer spending. While it is difficult for many Western people of my generation to get their minds around this, world shopping is being driven by the emerging world, with the BRICs the most important element.

A major part of the mental readjustment the developed world must undergo involves grasping the difference between wealth and size. Even as the BRICs grow rapidly in the coming years, Europeans and Americans will remain on a per capita basis considerably wealthier. With the possible exception of Russia, no BRIC country will achieve the same wealth as any of the G7 in the foreseeable future. Their gain does not imply our loss. So when Europeans tell me they are worried about competition from the BRICs, I ask them what it is they are really worried about. As I wrote earlier, the aggregate economic size of a country tends to be determined by the size of its working-age population and, crucially, their productivity. Short of enslaving other nations or encouraging mass immigration or somehow fostering an immediate and dramatic increase in birth rates, there is little that national leaders can do about their 'size'. If they focus on productivity, however, they can create a greater concentration of wealth among their citizens.

Switzerland does not worry about the growth of France, Germany and Italy. In fact, it wants them to grow, as it means the Swiss can export more and earn more income. The Swiss get richer on a per capita basis as their neighbours get richer. European countries should think about the BRIC countries in the same way, as export markets to be expanded for their own economic benefit.

Where absolute size tends to matter is in determining the role of countries in global institutions and in terms of defence, security and international affairs. In this regard, some of the current G7 members will have competitive issues as the BRICs' economies become bigger. It is critical that these developed countries don't hamper change purely because of blind national pride or as a way of preserving jobs in a bloated bureaucracy. Striving for optimal global solutions in areas beyond economics, including such fields as security and the environment, will allow the entire world to thrive and prosper.

If they are to improve the global institutions by properly including the BRICs, the developed countries and G7 members, especially the Europeans, are going to have to give up some of their power. This will require humility and a cold assessment of the facts. Japan and Europe no longer carry the relative weight they once did. The United States may soon have to share superpower status with China. How the established powers choose to accommodate the BRICs into global policymaking will determine whether they win or lose from this irreversible change in the world order.

7

New Allies Ahead

The rise of the BRIC economies and the Growth Markets will result in dramatic changes in relationships between those countries and the rest of the world, and regional economic and political ties will be subject to deep and lasting change. At times, this shift may test historical relationships between nations, but if policymakers can think openly and positively about the potential benefits of forging new trade and other links, it could be an opportunity for fresh and stronger alliances.

Take the huge increase in many countries' exports to the BRIC economies. Brazilian commodity exports to China have risen so much that China is now easily Brazil's number one export market. On the back of this, China's direct investments into Brazil are rising sharply. Both developments are leading to a new era of relations between the two countries. China's expanding investment into Africa is a similar exciting development, and raises the prospect of very different external relations for many African countries.

ASIAN AXIS

Asia's centrality to the future of the world economy makes it an obvious place to begin.

Within twenty years, China might be the world's biggest economy and India the third largest. More than two-thirds of the world's population is in Asia. In China and India, Asia has the world's only two economies with more than a billion inhabitants; their combined population is not far off 40 per cent of the world's current population. Indonesia, with around 240 million people, is the fourth most populous country. Japan, Bangladesh, Vietnam, Pakistan and the Philippines are among the top twenty populous countries. In total, six of the N-11 economies are in Asia, as, of course, are China and India. Taken together, the prospects for the continent are incredible.

For much of the period from the Second World War until 2010, Japan was the world's second largest economy. China has already overtaken Japan, and within twenty years so might India. The relative as well as absolute economic changes between China, India and Japan may necessitate a sea change in their interrelationships, made no easier by their chequered mutual history. This will require compromise and flexibility. In terms of coordination, Asia's leaders are going to have to be very tolerant and open-minded. Changes in relative wealth are unlikely to be quite as dramatic, but they will represent a considerable relative shift none the less.

Given all this, how is it possible to devise a healthy, peaceful economic, monetary and social relationship for Asia? How will the new giants, China and India, treat each other? What will be the regional role of the still prosperous but economically much smaller Japan? The same issue faces South Korea and all those large-population countries with great potential such as Bangladesh, Indonesia, the Philippines, Pakistan and Vietnam, and the smaller, more prosperous economies such as Singapore. What will happen to Taiwan? Will it become part of China as Hong Kong has? Hong Kong's 'Basic Law' protects the Hong Kong dollar only until the capital account of the balance of payments in China becomes open. If that happens, will the Hong Kong dollar cease to exist? What about North and South Korea? Will unification be helped or hindered by the BRICs' development and the changing landscape?

Beyond these commonly discussed issues are even bigger ones. The often fraught relationship between India and Pakistan could be tested even more by India's emergence as the world's third largest economy. Another complexity will be the relationship between China and Japan: can they forgive and forget the traumas of the past and move on to a healthy and compatible relationship as China becomes bigger – albeit less wealthy – than Japan? An even thornier issue could be the relationship between China and India.

These are all significant challenges for Asia's thought-leaders, who need to find ways of rising to them.

JAPAN AND THE BRICs

For Japan, the emergence of China is both a huge opportunity and a threat. With Japan's ageing demographics, it has often seemed to me that 'embracing' China could be a passport to a better economic future. The same is true with respect to India, and the huge markets that Indonesia and the other

N-11 economies offer. But it will require Japan to undergo quite dramatic cultural change.

Given Japan's technological prowess and its advanced stage of development, Japan has a lot of things to offer the Asian growth economies. Two areas are obvious, Japan's leadership in modern consumer appliances, ranging from autos to electronic appliances, as well as its leadership in modern energy efficiency. In recent years, it appears as though Germany is more successful in many areas of Chinese demand as consumers rise up the wealth ladder, with high-end cars being a particularly interesting example. Given the global leadership of Toyota in the auto industry, this should be a major opportunity. But relative to BMW and Mercedes, Japan's leading motor manufacturers don't seem to be quite seizing this opportunity. German brands are more popular in China. Japanese companies may suffer from the troubled history between the two countries. This is something that Japan is going to have to get beyond. It is arguably something that Germany has successfully achieved through the creation of the EU and European Monetary Union, which is why some advocate a monetary union for Asia. Commitment to this sort of powerful shift in the cultural and political relationship between China and Japan is the sort of step necessary for Japan to reap what appear to be huge potential benefits.

When I visit Tokyo I am often struck by how isolated Japan seems when faced with the changing dynamics of Asia. At a meeting I had with a leading Japanese consumer company strategy team a couple of years ago, I had expected them to be bursting with questions about China and India, but instead it was I who had to bring up the subject. I was quite astonished that they didn't emphasize the dramatic consumer opportunities which were on their doorstep. A market of 2.5 billion people or more – yet they didn't seem especially eager to exploit it. I've had similar experiences with other Japanese companies in different industries.

Another aspect of the Japan dilemma might be the use of English as a spoken language. How can Japan expect to exploit the potential benefits of China, India and beyond if they can't engage in a common language? At most of the meetings I'm part of in Japan there is a translator present. That used to be the case in Germany when I started in the financial services industry thirty years ago. Not today. If I give a speech in Frankfurt, I give it in English; the audience listens, understands and asks lots of questions – in English – at the end. In Tokyo there will be simultaneous translation and questions will usually be asked in Japanese.

In the past couple of years Japanese officials have embarked on a strategy to boost Japan's appeal as a tourist destination. I have travelled a little in Japan, and it is a beautiful and fascinating country. But for a non-Japanese speaker it is not an easy place to get around once you leave Tokyo and the train system. Embracing the English language would probably make it a lot easier for Japan to be successful in so many ways.

Similarly, more openness in Japan could help ameliorate the biggest problem the country faces: a dwindling labour force. What Japan needs is a major immigration strategy. Instead, whenever I raise the subject during my visits there, I am usually lectured about how foreign immigrant workers are responsible for the modest amount of crime that occurs in urban Japan. Japan must shift its attitudes if it is going to benefit from the rise of the BRICs and the N-11.

CHINA AND ITS ASIAN AMBITIONS

In addition to its relationship with Japan, China will need to develop a healthier relationship with the other BRICs. India will be especially important. China and India have experienced a chequered relationship and as they both become more important economically, they will have to develop a more positive dialogue.

Three areas seem especially important. Firstly, the scope for China and India to dramatically boost trade with each other is huge. In recent years it has started to accelerate significantly, but this is only the beginning. If China and India are set to become the biggest and third largest economies within the next twenty years, then their direct bilateral trade should become the largest trade relationship in the world, or close to it. Indeed, one might suggest that if Chinese–Indian bilateral trade does not rise dramatically, then they won't succeed in achieving their economic potential.

Secondly, China and India will be in direct competition for increasing quantities of global resources and their involvement in finding solutions to the predicaments of diminishing reserves and climate change is going to be critical. Of course, both countries are always going to put their own domestic economic interests first, but they will have to find a mutually acceptable stance for there to be a truly credible global agreement on climate change. It will probably be the case that enlightened self-interest will lead to both nations realizing that they face resource constraints. With bold and open-minded leaders, at some stage in the future this should present an opportunity for China and India to adopt a common stance.

Thirdly, the need for a common position between India and China is likely to extend beyond climate change. The future shape and stability of Pakistan is one example. The leadership, shape and role of global institutions such as the IMF, World Bank and possibly even the UN are all areas where China and India will have to try and explore common ground. Following the exit of Dominique Strauss-Kahn from the helm of the IMF in May 2011, the apparent lack of discussion between China and India on a suitable jointly desired candidate is something that will have to change. Today the US and Europe find it natural to debate and agree a common ground on global matters of mutual importance, and have done so for many years. China and India will need to do the same.

China's long-term stance on Taiwan and North Korea and its style of decision making is likely to have a major influence on its relationship with the rest of Asia as well as the US. Just as with the bilateral relationship with Japan, Chinese leaders may have to develop a different form of engagement to meet all these challenges. It won't be easy, but if China is going to achieve its potential, it will have to adapt.

ASIAN MONETARY AFFAIRS

Some academics suggest that, against this complex background, Asia should and will develop a single currency in the same way that the euro has developed at the core of the modern Europe. Many Asian thinkers have long dreamt of an Asian single currency, with some going as far as naming it the 'Acu', the Asian Currency Unit. The birth of the euro and the structure of European Monetary Union are regarded as an ideal model. The underlying comparison – closer economic and political cooperation born out of a desire not to repeat a troubled history – is understandable. But the differences between the relative size and structure of Asia's major economies add to the considerable complexities of developing a common currency.

A rush towards monetary union in Asia would be a highly risky pursuit. As the present crisis in Europe demonstrates, it is far from clear that the euro is successful in Europe. While there is little doubt whether technically the euro has functioned, there are doubts over whether the stability will persist and more importantly whether its existence will help deliver greater prosperity.

At the time of writing, the European Monetary Union (EMU) is under severe threat. While the immediate challenge is the degree of sovereign debt outstanding in Greece and some other smaller countries, in my judgement it is actually a test of the structure, governance and leadership of Europe. We can't have complete confidence that all the current member countries will stay in the eurozone, and for that matter whether a common currency has a long-term future. It will require very bold decision making from Europe's leaders.

This experience is important for those in Asia who are thinking about their own monetary futures, but there are differences between Asia and Europe, especially in terms of relative economic structures. Three things in particular are important.

Firstly, the 'core' countries which entered the EMU in 1999 – France, Germany and the Benelux – enjoyed a reasonably similar GDP per capita. At the beginning of the EMU, these countries perhaps were an optimal currency zone. The optimality of the EMU started to be questionable once it became clear that Spain, Portugal and Greece and, to some extent, Ireland, Italy and Finland would join. Introducing a single currency among China, India and Japan might be more akin to agreeing a single currency between Germany, Poland and Turkey, not the core group that was conceived for the EMU's creation. Japan has a GDP per capita of $36,000, China $6,000 and India $1,500. While China's and India's wealth will rise dramatically, it is tough to envisage them becoming as wealthy as Japan in the foreseeable future. Similarly, individual Indians are unlikely ever to become as wealthy as Chinese citizens.

Secondly, there are quite different patterns of trade relationships for the different major Asian economies as compared to the core members of the EMU. Most of the EMU member countries are significantly 'open' and their biggest trading partners were each other back in 1999. In creating the EMU, much of the goal was to create a common trade area and to reduce currency instability between the members. Within Asia the situation is different: for example, India is much less open to trade than China. A future Asian single currency based on the possible dominance of China and India might eventually be feasible, but this is not a given. While China has overtaken Japan as a trading partner for many Asian countries, Japan remains much more important than India. To introduce a single currency based on unstable trade relationships could be dangerous. Without more stable and more similar trade patterns, especially with each other, the case for a shared currency, at least economically, is not very strong.

The third factor relates to purpose and motive. France and Germany entered the concept of EMU with a common and strong desire to put in place an institutional framework that would avoid repeating historical conflicts, especially the two world wars of the twentieth century. In Asia, and especially between China and Japan, presumably there is a similar desire to avoid the aggression of the past, but does there exist the shared vision for the future that monetary reform involving China would require? Is it possible for a non-democratic country like China to consider seriously a monetary union with other nations? Perhaps China will have to evolve its system of politics and governance to encompass this possibility.

Given the complex issues surrounding Asia's structure, to cope with the ongoing rise of China and India, both absolutely and relatively, a pursuit of more flexible exchange rates combined with strengthened macroeconomic policies is likely to deliver more stable results. Enhanced flexibility of their foreign exchange policies in many Asian countries, together with the adoption of credible inflation targeting regimes, are likely to help deliver greater stability. If China and India give more formal weight to inflation targets it will enhance their chances of sustained growth. Korea, of course, already practises inflation targeting and it seems likely that the Bank of Japan will move closer to a more formal inflation targeting framework at some stage. Against a background of inflation targeting, these big four countries should allow their exchange rates to move against each other, and against the dollar and the euro. Occasional central bank intervention to smooth out excessive currency fluctuations would be sensible, but to try to fix their exchange rates against each other seems an unhelpful pursuit.

If in a few decades the big developing economies have reached their potential, then perhaps stronger efforts to move towards a shared currency may be more sensible. Until then, given the divergent pressures that are liable to persist in their economies, it will probably remain too ambitious a goal.

*

Of course, the feasibility and structure of any future Asian monetary system will depend crucially on what happens to the renminbi. If China reaches its economic potential in the next twenty to thirty years, and if it has allowed full convertibility, under which there would be no restrictions on the use of the renminbi, either for Chinese individuals and businesses or for anyone else around the world conducting any transaction with China, then it is quite likely that the renminbi will sit at the heart of global monetary affairs and not just those of Asia. While Chinese policymakers are always very careful not to commit to any timetable, it seems as though there is a commitment on the part of the Chinese government to full convertibility. Indeed without the renminbi being freely accessible in terms of trade and capital flows between China and the rest of the world, it is not obvious that China can reach its other stated goals – in particular the desire for Shanghai to be a leading international financial centre. While many international companies show an interest in listing their equity on the Shanghai stock market, unless they can be more comforted that investors would be able to buy and sell with the same general laws that are associated with stock exchanges in the West, then many will be reluctant.

During 2010 and early 2011 there were some initiatives to open up the use of the renminbi for investment purposes in Hong Kong. These hint at the ultimate potential for the renminbi. The growth in renminbi-denominated deposits in Hong Kong since 2009 has been remarkable, and is set to grow a lot more.

For other Asian economies, especially those with large tradable-goods sectors, the logical path is active exchange rate policy management against a basket of the big three currencies of China, Japan and India (combined with some reference to the dollar and euro). This would be applicable to Indonesia, Malaysia, the Philippines, Thailand, Vietnam and other countries in Asia.

THE BRICs AND THE US

While the most thrilling aspects of the BRICs story lie in Asia, the dynamics involving the US are nearly as complicated and exciting. How will the world's only superpower continue to deal with the prospect of losing this mantle, especially to a 'communist' regime in China? How will the US manage its Asian relationships? Will Japan remain its pre-eminent geopolitical partner in the East as it has been for much of the modern era, despite its relative decline? Or will the US 'drop' Japan? How should the US support the emergence of Russia without dramatic changes in how the Kremlin presides over business and general life in Russia? And what about Latin America, in which Brazil and Mexico may emerge as more forceful voices on the global scene? Finally, and probably key to the answer to all these questions: how will the US economy cope with the collective BRIC challenge?

Despite the threat to its sole dominant world leadership, many signs suggest that US policymakers are coping admirably with the emergence of the BRICs, allowing the economic forces of globalization to benefit their globally minded companies and thereby supporting an environment in which the BRICs can emerge. It also often seems as though US policymakers are at the forefront of those willing to include the BRIC economies in global dialogue. Certainly, the revival of the G20 in late 2008 by President Bush was a major step in bringing the BRIC countries to the centre of global policymaking. At the same time, the US has been eager to develop stronger bilateral dialogue, especially with each of China and India.

Such an open-minded approach from US leaders is sensible in view of the changing patterns of US trade relationships. The scale of the changes in US trade can be seen from looking at a number of indicators. For example, the Federal Reserve Board has an index to measure the performance of the dollar against all the US trade partners. It is calculated on the basis of both direct bilateral trade with each other and trade in markets other than their own. The Chinese currency now carries a weight that is as important as the Japanese yen. The combined weight of the renminbi and the Mexican peso is already greater than the euro, and the aggregate weight of G7 currencies is not much beyond 50 per cent.

During the next five years the most important goal of US economic policy will be to double its exports and reduce its large foreign debt. If the US is to succeed in reversing its balance of payments deficit, managing the trade relationships with the BRIC economies is vital.

And managing the relationship with China is especially important. They are the two biggest economies in the world and are likely to remain so for at least the next twenty to thirty years. Trade between the two economies is likely to rise significantly. Their stance on matters of global economic importance will be key to a prosperous world, as will their stance on matters of global security and political issues. It is going to be more and more vital that US citizens are educated objectively about China. The two countries are going to have to find successful ways of cooperating. After all, the US is the world's largest democratic economy and China is the world's biggest non-democratic economy. Many US citizens have been educated to believe that democracy is the only model that can deliver success.

China is challenging that wisdom. At a time when the US economy is struggling, it is easy to blame others, and especially China. It is highly fashionable for US politicians to blame China for America's economic problems. Proposals to introduce policies to restrict Chinese exports are often circulating in congressional committees. These ideas are probably wrong. Many US multinational companies have been at the forefront of helping China export to the US. This has benefited US consumers in terms of cheaper products and higher living standards. Walmart's growth typifies this reality.

But things are changing. As China develops and becomes wealthier, it will cease to be a source of cheap imports. In fact, it is becoming an ever larger recipient of other countries' exports. In 2010 Chinese imports rose to $1.4 trillion, an increase of $400 billion in just twelve months. If this pace is maintained, then by 2015 China's dollar value of imports will be bigger than America's. This is a huge opportunity for US exporters. Members of the US Congress have to resist the temptation to blame China for lost jobs in key marginal states simply to attract superficially easy votes. It will be better to look to the opportunity.

Of course, just as US politicians need to keep 'open minds' in the pursuit of more and freer global trade, the BRIC countries have to recognize the need for more 'free' economic policies, especially regarding exchange rates. As I have said, it was impressive that President Bush moved to bring the BRIC countries into the G20, so solutions could be found for complex economic problems. From a US perspective, increasing world trade with the BRICs together with increased flexibility of BRIC and Asian currencies (China's in particular) is a likely goal. US leadership on these issues is highly important for the continued benefits of globalization, not just for the US, but for us all.

Some US citizens may be scared of the challenge and competitive threat posed by China and the BRICs. To them I would again emphasize the difference between wealth and size. It is very unlikely that the BRIC economies will see their wealth get close to US levels in the foreseeable future, even if the size of some of these economies surpasses the US. If China's GDP gets to $80 trillion by 2050, the US will become $36 trillion. The US will still treble in size and its wealth probably double or more. Individual American citizens will earn around $94,000 each, making them nearly twice as rich as the Chinese and four times as rich as their Indian counterparts.

In 2006 the OECD studied different measures of 'success', and concluded that well-being appeared to correlate highly with GDP per capita. If China, India and the other BRICs become large economies it will be because of the size of their working population rather than per capita GDP. The US has prospered despite the decline of its manufacturing industry for many years. There is no reason why this trend can't continue. In fact it is quite possible that the US could even reverse this decline in manufacturing. If the US were to succeed in doubling exports over the next five years, it is likely that manufacturing will benefit disproportionately. The Boston Consulting Group (BCG) published a highly important report in May 2011 showing it is possible that the US will completely restore lost manufacturing competitiveness versus China in the next five years.[1]

When I discuss US manufacturing and exports with many financial market professionals, they think that this sort of idea is wildly fanciful. I think that such scepticism is not justified. With the competitiveness offered by the decline in the dollar and the growth in demand in the BRIC countries, the US has an opportunity to rebuild its domestic manufacturing capacity.

THE US, BRAZIL AND LATIN AMERICA

It occasionally seems that because of the security and terrorist threats emanating from the Middle East, and the excitement surrounding Asia, the US is no longer either as interested in or as influential in Latin America as it once was. Latin America's repeated economic crises, while Asia boomed from the late 1990s onwards, added to the perception.

It will be interesting to see whether this changes as Brazil's economy continues to get bigger. Brazil, already drawn more to China because of trade, sees itself firmly at the centre of the BRIC political club and is less needy of Washington. It may also see its influence grow throughout Latin America. Past Brazilian goals such as Mercosur, a common market of South American countries, may reappear as major priorities. For US policymakers, ensuring a healthy and vibrant trade relationship with Latin America as a whole will involve staying highly engaged with Brazil.

The bilateral meeting between President Obama and President Dilma Rousseff in March 2011 was a positive sign that the US realizes Brazil is embarking on a different, more prosperous path, and one that could be good for America.

Developments in China may have an extremely important bearing for Mexico. It is often noted how poorly Mexico has performed relative to Brazil as the BRIC story has unfolded. One credible reason is that China's appearance as a major low-cost production centre reduced the attraction of Mexico for US companies. As China becomes wealthier, its wages rise and its living standards improve it is conceivable that Mexico could be a big winner.

THE US AND RUSSIA

In terms of Russia there are three broad issues that matter for the US relationship: oil, politics and Europe.

Firstly, oil. Given the insatiable global appetite for energy and the persistent Middle Eastern troubles, Russia is important to the US as a key energy player. Its oil production strategy and the resulting implications for energy prices matter. Since the collapse of the Berlin Wall in 1989, Washington often seems eager to try to observe Russia in a positive light, despite their volatile relationship. Now with Russian oil and natural gas at least in theory open to the influence of world market dynamics, the US has a natural interest in engaging with Russia.

The second issue that will frame the US relationship, linked to the oil issue, is of course politics, and the structure of the US and Russian societies. Since the Cold War days, the Russian political ideology has been a topic of importance to American leaders irrespective of whether Democrats or Republicans were in power. Many US politicians remember the Soviet Union and being raised in that era. They are mindful of any signs of a reversion to those days in terms of Russian governance or, more importantly, engagement with the rest of the world. As the Russian economy grows and individuals prosper, the US obviously has a big role to play in encouraging this trend, especially in terms of helping Russian politics become more open. The complexities of this interplay will inevitably increase with Russia's success. The US may need to adopt a more imaginative approach to some of their differences of opinion. Quite often it seems as though Russia and the aspirations of its citizens are seen by US citizens in a very 'black and white' framework. There often seems to be a presumption that Russians would like to enjoy a similar society to that of the US. But in my view Russians want wealth and power; American-style democracy doesn't seem high on the agenda. Understanding the mentality of Russians will remain an important concern for the US.

This brings me to the third factor, which I will discuss in greater depth in the context of the challenges Europe faces vis-à-vis the BRICs. If Russia does become as big as Germany in terms of GDP per capita as well as in absolute size, it is highly probable that the US may need to rethink aspects of its overall relationship with its post-war allies in Europe. The whole nature of the European Union may need to change if Russia becomes as large as its potential suggests. Indeed, Russia might, one day, be a candidate to become a member of the EU. The US is highly likely to want to play a role in influencing any such development.

EUROPE AND THE BRICs

It is a popular perception among Europeans that Europe can only lose from the BRICs' success. This is a peculiar mindset, and is among Europe's greatest barriers to future economic progress. In many ways, it reflects a more common European concern that somehow Europe can no longer influence the rest of the world, and can only be influenced by it. Changing this perception and raising the awareness that the emergence of the BRICs can be a positive for Europe is an urgent task for Europe's political leaders and intellectual thinkers. Part of the problem is that three of the four BRIC countries are distant from Europe. The distance breeds unfamiliarity. The challenge posed by the emergence of China as the most important BRIC is particularly tough. And even though Russia is geographically closer, or at least Moscow and St Petersburg, its major cities of influence, are, this brings its own problems and opportunities.

The four BRIC countries are also viewed differently by different countries in Europe. This in itself adds to the task of turning the BRICs' potential from a threat to a collective opportunity. In those European countries with less sophisticated economies, China has long been an important competitor in various manufacturing industries. On the other hand, in larger and more sophisticated economies, where services comprise a larger proportion of output, India may be seen as providing more competition than China. However, it is important that all European leaders work hard to persuade their populations that the emergence of the BRICs and their ability to fulfil their potential is something that will be good for the whole continent. While many low-value-added manufacturing countries think they lose out to China in terms of manufacturing, a quick glance at Germany shows how this perception does not need to be true. Domestic German industrial production is thriving. Exports are at the heart of this strength.

The top German car makers have seen enormous growth

in their business in the BRIC countries, as have some of the heavier industrial companies, including those in the chemical industry. A day spent visiting the famous companies of Munich can leave you with an impression that what is going on in China is more important than anything happening in the rest of Europe, or indeed possibly in many parts of Germany. Of course, there are some important complications that arise from these changing trade patterns, including the importance of EMU to German companies.

Europe's individual citizens as consumers should play a more forceful role in trying to welcome the competition from the BRIC economies. It would mean cheaper consumer goods, which would allow the budgets of European households to be spread more effectively and so give rise to stronger consumption. Europeans should be happy to 'trade' better, more productive jobs with lower inflation for the less-efficient industries it can afford to lose to the BRICs and other emerging economies. Indeed, it is easy to observe in recent years that the individual European countries that are prepared to allow cheap imports from the developing world are typically the same countries that have frequently seen positive inflation surprises, and in many cases stronger economic growth.

This is almost definitely not a fluke but a function of sound economic policy. The whole rationale of international trade is that it is for the benefit of both sides. International trade is not a zero sum game, and our political leaders need to understand its benefits and explain it to all of their citizens.

Europe often seems to struggle more than the US in responding to today's changing world economy. An appropriate collective response is pretty straightforward, at least on paper. Allow the EU and EMU to function. As a common economic zone, the twenty-seven-member EU has a population much bigger than the US, which gives it scope to be bigger economically. The potential consumer market is so vast that it should be easy to accommodate the emergence of four BRICs. If the EU were allowed to operate as a genuine free economic trade area, then the resulting benefits would be highly significant.

Free trade with external non-European countries, especially the BRICs, should be not only tolerated but encouraged. Within the EU legislative policies are necessary to complete the single market, in particular for service industries. To complement this EU member countries must allow cross-border mergers to accelerate, allowing more efficient international business. Unfair domestic regulatory support of national champions should be strongly discouraged. Free movement of labour and enhanced flexibility of wage agreements needs to advance significantly. Improved steps to allow immigration between EU members and from outside are also necessary. Supplementing labour, especially skilled labour, will be necessary to help business in view of the inevitable decline in the indigenous labour force in many European countries. Policies to raise the retirement age and allow people to work longer are vital. As people are likely to live longer, this would expand the labour pool as well as reducing the dependency ratio which otherwise looms as a massive challenge.

In such a bolder, braver environment, my guess is that it would be likely that the BRICs' emergence as major economic actors would be regarded more as an opportunity than a threat.

EU RELATIONS WITH RUSSIA

Of the challenges posed by the BRICs, that of Russia to Europe is perhaps the most interesting because the two share a border. There could be a case for allowing Russia to eventually join the EU or some future version of it. Of course, geographically large parts of Russia sit in Asia, but if Russia is to achieve its potential, surely a positive minded Europe should seek to welcome the country into the EU. Of course, the same could be said of Turkey.

Russia is going to remain a major energy source for much of the EU, both its old enemies and some countries that used to be part of the Soviet empire. This factor alone suggests an ongoing need for EU countries to pursue good relations with Russia, despite tendencies for the relationship frequently to become tense.

Russia is an important trading partner for many EU members and if Russia is going to grow to the size of its potential, it will become an even bigger export market for those countries. This is where the economic rationale for Russia to become part of an EU economic zone is substantial. The case for the EU's and the EMU's existence rests largely on the amount of trade between member countries. If Russia remains as important in terms of trade and fulfils its BRIC potential, then including Russia inside the EU would make a great deal of economic sense.

Whether Russia would want to join it is another matter. (Norway and Switzerland both manage to thrive within Europe despite being outside the EU.) Given its history and frequently different political philosophy, Russia might prefer to be outside. Gaining economic clout may add to Russia's desire to stay as a powerful independent voice in world affairs. This in itself would be reason for the EU (and the US) to encourage a different way of thinking. It will become increasingly fascinating as and when Russia emerges as a more powerful economy.

EUROPE AND THE REST OF THE BRICs

China is currently the most important of the other BRIC countries so far as Europe is concerned, despite its distant location, because of its major importance in terms of rising trade with Europe.

It is notable how much more focused on the topic of monetary reform European policymakers have become in the past couple of years. While EU policymakers don't attract the media headlines enjoyed by US politicians, they share an obsession with the need for the significant appreciation of China's currency. Future efforts towards global monetary reform are emerging, as evidenced by the stance adopted by the French during their presidency of the G20 in the first half of 2011. In March, President Sarkozy and his team had proposed a meeting of all G20 members and used the opportunity to promote the idea of a different monetary system in the future. Suggesting that the meeting should be hosted in China was a clever symbolic statement of the French belief that the renminbi has a role to play.

As for Brazil, its strongest trading relationships are with Spain and Portugal – so if Brazil fulfils its BRIC potential then it will be of economic benefit to both these countries. Some Spanish- and Portuguese-based multinationals are heavily exposed to business in Brazil (as well as in other Latin

American countries) and this could be very helpful to them in the future. Given the relatively developed nature of Brazil's capital markets, it is quite likely that financial institutions in Europe will be looking to explore other opportunities in Brazil.

In order to adapt successfully to the changing conditions resulting from the rise of the BRICs – and the other Growth Markets – it is vital that nations actively share policies to support the smooth operation of rising international trade. It's also crucial to move towards a better structure of global economic governance or, it might be said, a new world order.

8

A New World Order

Back in 2001 it was obvious to me that the institutional framework for running the world economy needed an overhaul. When I coined the acronym BRICs I argued that the G7, G8 and IMF were no longer suitable entities to deal with the challenges of the new world. Today it is even more obvious.

There is more than national or political pride at stake here. Unless the BRICs are embraced more fully by the powers that now dominate the world's economic policy councils, we cannot enjoy the full benefits of their growth. Those countries which ran the world for the latter half of the twentieth century cannot afford to be squeamish or judgemental about countries which now rival them economically, just because of their different social and political systems.

If we genuinely wish to pull more people out of poverty into the middle class and facilitate greater trade and wealth creation, then we need to think hard about overcoming the obstacles which still hinder the free flow of commerce. International economic governance is no longer just a subject to excite economists; it is a vital element of the way the world works today, and one that affects us all.

*

The G6 club of the richest and largest industrialized countries was founded in 1975 when the then US President, Gerald Ford, convened a summit to discuss the first oil price crisis. He invited Japan, the UK, Germany, France and Italy to talks with the United States. In 1976 he added Canada, to balance the large European contingent, thus forming the G7. Collectively these countries dominated world trade at the time. The initial 1975 meeting was intended as a 'one off' purely to deal with a coordinated response to the oil price crisis. But once Canada was added, G7 summits became a permanent feature of the international economic policy calendar. The countries' finance ministers and central bank governors still, typically, meet three or four times each year.

As large economies with reasonably similar income levels per head and shared democratic values, the G7 countries are vaguely similar. But they are hardly representative of the world economy in the way they were back in the 1980s. Back then, China was economically irrelevant. Today it is the second largest economy in the world. Brazil is bigger now than Italy. France, Germany and Italy share a single currency. Each of Brazil, India and Russia is bigger than Canada. Yet the G7 still meet and their leaders still behave as though their nations dominate the world.

If the G7 were being formed today it would have to include China. A case could easily be made for Brazil, India or Russia over Canada, and since the introduction of the euro as a common currency in 1999, there seems little logic behind the individual participation of three eurozone members in the G7, especially the smallest of them, Italy.

If membership hinged only on economic criteria rather than political influence, then I would suggest that a new 'Growth 8' grouping comprising the Growth Markets would be a much more sensible club than the G7. From 2011 to 2020, the change in the aggregate GDP of the 'Growth 8' is likely to be around double that of the G7 in US-dollar terms. China alone might match the G7's contribution to global growth.

In 1998, the G7 Heads of State Summit did adjust to a changing world, when it invited Russia to make up a G8 following the rouble crisis. Washington encouraged the invitation, at a moment when the Americans still hoped Boris Yeltsin would lead Russia towards free markets and democracy. Neither materialized in the way the G7 had hoped. But despite this experience, the G7 must find an appropriate forum in which world policymakers can meet regularly in an effective manner to implement better solutions to the economic challenges of our times. The days of a 'Western' club of democracies is well past its sell-by date. Perhaps the G20 is – for now – the best we can come up with.

The G20 members include nineteen of the world's largest economies plus the European Union, as well as the heads of the IMF and World Bank. It first met in 1999, following the Asian financial crisis in 1997–8, then lay more or less dormant for a decade before its stature was enhanced in 2008, when President George W. Bush, a man not widely seen as an enthusiastic advocate of global economic cooperation, called for a meeting of its leaders to discuss the global credit crisis. As of now, it has become the most representative group to discuss truly global economic issues. It may include more members than is ideal for frequent decision making but it has more legitimacy than the (still influential) G7, as it includes the BRIC countries.

In June 2004 Bob Hormats – vice chairman at Goldman Sachs who went on to become Under Secretary of State for Economic,

Energy and Agricultural Affairs at the US State Department – and I jointly wrote a paper calling for three reforms to the G7 and G20 system: the formation of a 'Financial 8', adding China to the G7 finance ministers; a more substantial role for the G20; and a move to reduce the representation of the continental European members, France, Germany and Italy, to one from three.[1] (If the latter were agreed, we argued the F8 would then reduce back to an F6, a much more powerful group.) In 2006, Edwin Truman of the Peterson Institute for International Economics (IIE) wrote a paper suggesting that the G20 had strong global legitimacy.[2] He argued that most of them could be described as 'Systemically Important Countries', countries whose economic performance and policies affect the global economy and the stability of the global financial system, and whose active or passive policies had effects far beyond their own borders. Ted argued that they needed to be held responsible for their activities in the world, in return for which they needed appropriate representation. The G20, he wrote, might be the best forum for giving them the voice their economic weight merited.

In his paper Truman showed that from 2000 to 2005, the G20 contributed around 77 per cent of world nominal GDP with the non-industrial countries contributing more than the G7, 42.7 per cent vs. 34 per cent. The lion's share of the non-industrialized countries' contribution came from the BRICs, as it still does. The G20 not only includes the BRICs, but also several members of both our Growth Markets group, and the Next Eleven, such as Korea, Indonesia, Mexico and Turkey. Based on Truman's definition of Systemically Important Countries, it is easy to conceive of a world in which other N-11 countries such as Egypt, the Philippines and Nigeria achieve the status of Growth Markets, representing at least

1 per cent of global GDP, and deserve greater global representation.

While there are a number of countries hammering on the doors of the 'G' groups, another persistent problem is ushering out those countries whose relevance has waned. Once a country has been admitted to a G group, it is hard to force it out again. I have often thought that a major task for the IMF should be setting eligibility criteria for G groups. There should be a system of promotion and relegation based on clear objective indicators. Criteria could include size, wealth and perhaps something akin to a GES which measures sustainable progress.

It would be a tough diplomatic challenge for the IMF or anyone to manage the national egos and force implementation of such an approach, but if successful, it would make the G groups consistently relevant and manageable. The prospect of membership could also serve to motivate countries such as Pakistan, Iran and Nigeria. The idea that under certain conditions they could be part of the club running global affairs might become a powerful incentive, in the same way that EU membership was coveted by the former Soviet states of eastern Europe.

Right now, I hear from many G20 officials and their staff that the meetings of the group are so demanding that they are left with little time for anything else. Especially for smaller European countries such as the Netherlands, the status and influence acquired by being part of the G20 impose enormous bureaucratic demands. While more legitimate than the G7 or G8 in terms of its wider membership, it is not clear that the G20 is more effective.

Finding this balance between legitimacy and effectiveness is an ongoing problem for any global organization. The Japanese earthquake in March 2011 offered an interesting case study. Immediately after the earthquake, the Japanese yen inexplicably, and probably unjustifiably, started to rise, punishing Japan's exporters at their moment of greatest weakness. It was the G7, not the G20, who came to Japan's aid, intervening in the currency markets to drive down the yen.

The G7 acted because it was easier and quicker than trying to involve all the G20 countries. What would be ideal would be an organization with the legitimacy of the G20 but the decisiveness and flexibility of the G7. Once again there would be guidelines for changing membership, adjusting for economic reality, and the mechanisms for making timely financial interventions in the world economy.

As a basic criterion for membership in the G20, I would like to see only countries of significant economic scale, accounting for at least 1 per cent of global GDP, represented. This would allow in all the current G7 members, the defined Growth Markets, and others such as Australia and Spain. South Africa, Argentina and Saudi Arabia, all of whom are current G20 members, would just miss out. Additional reference points for membership might be introduced, such as per capita wealth and level of development. To ensure that the group could be effective, a more legitimate G7 (or F8) could be established, to operate in emergencies, within or under the G20 umbrella.

As noted, one obvious step towards streamlining the management of the G7 and G20 would be merging the memberships of France, Germany and Italy into a single EU common currency membership. When the G7 intervened to restrain the yen in March 2011, it was the European Central Bank which operated in the foreign exchange markets, not the central banks of the individual countries. Since France,

Germany and Italy now have a common currency and a common monetary policy, it seems simply through force of habit that they attend global economic meetings as separate entities. Moreover, as I often find myself thinking during periods of intense crisis for the European Monetary Union, it would send an extremely powerful signal to world financial markets if its three key members acted with one voice, with a single EU finance minister and the ECB president attending G7 meetings.

Canadian and British membership of the G7 might also soon come under scrutiny, but I see nothing wrong with that. Political pride might lead them to argue that exclusion from the G7 would diminish them internationally and economically. But I would disagree. Switzerland plays no role in the G7, and yet its currency is more important than Canada's and Zurich is a more important financial centre than Toronto. Geneva, Zurich, and even Singapore are more important than Italy's financial centres in Milan and Rome.

Taking this streamlined vision even further, I can see a good argument for an even smaller group, a G4 and F4, made up of the EMU group, the US, China and Japan, to manage global economic affairs at least for the next few years. Certainly China would have made a more potent participant in the recent yen intervention than Canada or the UK.

The BRICs, however, are not just standing by waiting to be invited by the traditional economic powers to join one or other of their clubs. In 2009 their leaders decided to hold their first summit. They met, at the invitation of Russia, in Yekaterinburg in June of that year for two days. I was delighted to see an acronym I had created evolve into a rival to the G7. They met again in 2011, with South Africa added to the mix. My own invitations to the events must have got lost in the post.

On one level I cannot see the rationale for this new political club. The BRICs all have large populations, and are likely to be the dominant influence on the global economy in the decades ahead. But beyond that they are very different. In terms of people India and China, with more than a billion, dwarf the other two. In terms of GDP, China is nearly three times as big as Brazil, and close to four times the size of India and Russia. In terms of per capita wealth, Brazil and Russia are currently of similar wealth and both much richer than China, with India lagging far behind. China matters to all the BRICs, but aside from that, they don't matter so much to each other. It is not obvious to me that they have the common interests or common attributes that benefit from a regular mutual club-type association.

The G7 countries have many more shared characteristics, including the fact that they are all well-developed democracies. Brazil and India have democratic political structures, but China and Russia do not. The addition of South Africa to the BRIC group in 2011 only adds to the confusion. Compared to the BRICs, it has a small population and small GDP. A better case could have been made for any of the other four Growth Markets. If it was seen as necessary to have an African member, Nigeria might have been an equally suitable candidate. South Africa appears to have been included because of its commodity prowess, but do the BRIC leaders want theirs to be a club of commodity producers?

Whatever the future of the global monetary system – and I hope it comes to reflect the tilt in economic influence – it remains very unlikely that a BRIC single currency will ever be adopted. The euro, for all its problems, serves a group of economies which are similar in terms of structure, wealth and shared political beliefs. The argument for the monetary union of France, Austria, the Benelux countries and the former West Germany was well founded. It became less convincing when expanded to include less wealthy countries, such as Portugal and Greece. But at least they were on the same continent. There is no similar logic for an everyday BRIC currency, unless of course it was part of a newly constructed and expanded Special Drawing Right, incorporating the world's other major currencies, which I shall consider in more detail later in the chapter.

All of this being said, I can still see good reasons for the BRIC countries to meet alone these days – if only to show how ridiculous it is to keep excluding them from the G7, and to limit their influence at the IMF, the World Bank, even the United Nations. These are big countries in terms of population and size, and together are increasingly the marginal driver of world growth. They have a shared interest in the future of the global monetary system, and when they meet they discuss the increasing convertibility of their currencies and cross-border trade.

These issues affect the entire world and the BRICs deserve fitting representation at the major international councils. To achieve this they cannot just wait for the current incumbents to make way or invite them in. They need to seize the influence their size demands.

For now, at least, the G7 members are much more effective at high politics. In May 2011, for example, after Dominique Strauss-Kahn was forced to resign from the IMF, battle was engaged to choose his successor. The European countries quickly mobilized behind the French finance minister, Christine

Lagarde, who embarked on a world tour to win support. The BRIC-nation leaders did not adopt a collective stance; indeed, they all appeared to have their own preferences, although their preferences were not always made public. Although many commentators opined that the Europeans should no longer regard the managing directorship of the IMF as their right, there was in fact little opposition from the BRICs or elsewhere. Since the end of the Second World War, when the International Monetary Fund and the World Bank were established, the head of the IMF has been European and the head of the World Bank American, reflecting the division of economic power in the middle of the twentieth century. But this is clearly now an anachronism. The heads of the IMF and the World Bank should now be decided on merit, not nationality.

An effective head of the IMF or the World Bank must be technically capable of leading those organizations and, therefore, expert in economic matters. An effective head also needs to be skilled in negotiating with all its constituent members. I've heard it said that there are no suitable BRIC candidates for such difficult jobs. I disagree. Brazil's former central bank governor, Arminio Fraga, and India's deputy planning minister, Montek Singh Ahluwalia, would both be excellent candidates. Similarly, while not from a BRIC country, Mexico's central bank governor, Agustín Carstens, seems very capable, as of course does Israel's Stanley Fischer, formerly a senior official at the IMF.

The difficulties of appointing a Chinese head of the IMF were brought home to me at a Goldman Sachs BRIC event during the search for a successor to Strauss-Kahn. I was on a panel with Peter Sutherland, an Irish politician, businessman and former director general of the World Trade Organization, and Martin Wolf of the *Financial Times*. We were asked if we thought it was fitting for China to provide the next head of the IMF, given that it is not a democracy. Martin and Peter thought not. I was more equivocal. Since a country doesn't need to be a democracy to join the IMF, why should officials from certain member countries be barred from serving at its highest level? Running an international institution based in Washington DC might prove a shock to someone raised within the Communist Party of China, but it would certainly not be impossible. And as China gets bigger and its global influence becomes greater and clearer, this will probably change. A future head of the IMF from China or any BRIC country must surely be a possibility.

For it to happen, the BRICs will have to become more politically astute. After Strauss-Kahn's resignation, many in the BRIC countries talked about how unfair it was that the Europeans regarded the IMF as their fiefdom, yet they failed to come up with a mutually acceptable candidate to challenge Lagarde. While I repeat that the main criterion is that a head must be effective, irrespective of domicile, the fact that the BRIC countries could not decide on a joint candidate points to the limitations, at least currently, of the BRIC political club.

The IMF and the World Bank will also need to transform themselves to reflect the new world order. In the 1990s the IMF's austere policy advice to troubled Asian economies was harsh and possibly inappropriate. It scarred its reputation, and left it looking biased towards European and US interests. Sir Mervyn King, the governor of the Bank of England, made a powerful speech in India in 2006 arguing for radical reforms at the IMF. He said that unless the IMF invited India and China directly into central, global policymaking, it risked losing both its legitimacy and its relevance. He made several specific recommendations, among them that the IMF should improve its analysis of the appropriate net external asset and/or liability balance-sheet position of its members in order that advance awareness of vulnerability to external shocks be enhanced and that it should be much more bold and directive in recommending appropriate exchange rates for them. Only then could the IMF claim a significant role in rectifying the vast imbalances building up on the world's balance sheets.

Edwin Truman of the IIE went even further in his paper, recommending a shake-up of the IMF executive, reducing the number of European Union member seats from ten to one, admitting more countries from Asia and Africa and adjusting voting rights and shares in IMF articles accordingly. Collectively these measures would create a stronger, more dynamic IMF, capable of issuing credible, respected recommendations for enhancing the world's monetary and exchange rate system over time.

In 2009, provoked by the credit crisis, the G20 leaders met and agreed the basis for a new set of voting rights and ownership structure of the IMF. By the end of 2010, specific changes were agreed and by 2013 those changes should have been implemented. China's share of the voting rights will rise to just above 6 per cent, the third highest, just behind Japan. Each of the other BRIC countries will be in the top ten, reasonably consistent with the rising share of the world economy that each enjoys. In some ways, this is major progress, certainly compared with the days before the credit crisis, but whether the Fund can continue to adapt to the pace of the rise of the BRIC economic story remains to be seen. To some extent, that will depend both on whether the BRIC economies rise as I expect and on their own leadership. Changing the IMF's leadership to reflect these dynamic changes should remain one of the organization's top priorities.

As the BRICs and the other Growth Markets become ever more intertwined with the rest of the world, their political leaders will exert ever more influence on the global monetary system and their demands from it will be increasingly relevant. But at the same time their internal stability will continue to be paramount. Their ability to control inflation, and thus keep their citizens happy, will partly depend on what they choose to do about their currency regimes. For example, as China becomes more successful and developed, it will have to take inflation even more seriously. This means it probably will have less focus on keeping the value of the renminbi stable, and certainly not at the expense of domestic inflation management. In recent years, keeping it artificially stable against the dollar – by purchasing huge amounts of foreign currency – has kept China's exports humming along. But as China develops and its people's wealth and aspirations grow, the government will probably have to allow its currency to fluctuate more. This will not mean that the Chinese economy will have to suddenly become unstable, any more than the UK, the euro area or the US as the pound, the euro and the dollar move up and down against each other. Keeping internal prices under control is a much more important measure of stability than the external value of the currency.

China is probably worried about a world where it could lose control of its exchange rate. Anyone who has endured a currency crisis can tell you how miserable it is. Interest rates soar, inflation takes hold and suddenly the dry technicalities of money supply dominate political discussion.

But despite the occasional crisis, the current floating

exchange-rate system has coped well with the immense challenges and crises that the world has been through since 1971–3, when the Bretton Woods system was abandoned. That system had been implemented after the Second World War to regulate the international monetary system through managed exchange rates. When it ended, the major currencies were allowed to float freely against each other, and this system survived the 1970s oil price rises, the 1980s Latin American international debt crisis, the late 1980s to early 1990s turbulence within the European Monetary Union, the Asian crisis of 1997, the collapse of the Long Term Capital Management hedge fund, the bursting of the internet bubble in 2000–1 and, most recently, the global credit crisis of 2007–8. While major currencies have periods of volatility, they have broadly followed a predictable path.

Since I joined Goldman Sachs in 1995, my preferred methodology for understanding exchange rate movements has been to assume that, over time, exchange rates will reflect countries' purchasing power parity (PPP) adjusted for their relative productivity performance. The GSDEER – Goldman Sachs Dynamic Equilibrium Exchange Rate – currency model that I developed was based on this premise. The core idea here is that, given certain inputs, currencies should trade at certain prices relative to each other. I then adjust this index to reflect the relative productivity in the different currency zones.

As I explained earlier, under PPP the price of a cup of coffee in New York converted into euros should buy a cup of coffee in Paris. In a more productive economy, the cup of coffee should cost a little less, as the inputs for making and serving it are used more efficiently. Relative productivity thus helps explain demand for a particular currency. Less productive countries tend to have weaker currencies and vice versa. The performance of the US dollar against other major currencies through time reflects the fact that US productivity continues to outperform that of most other major nations, thereby attracting the capital flows necessary to offset the current account deficit. Of course, there are movements around this equilibrium both up and down – a lot of the latter for the dollar in recent years – reflecting cyclical economic developments. But the underlying trends are nearly always driven by relative prices and productivity.

GSDEER has helped me understand currency movements. From the 1970s onwards, the yen came under strong pressure to appreciate against the dollar and other world currencies. The Japanese economy was strengthening and becoming much more productive. From the mid-1990s onwards, however, its growth slowed sharply and its relative productivity lost its edge. Since then, the equilibrium exchange rate between the yen and the dollar has stabilized, and until the global credit crisis it had become a much less volatile and directional trade. Of course, in the past couple of years, the yen has once again strengthened, although this time it seems unjustified, based on a GSDEER approach. The yen's newfound strength appears to be a reflection of simply a weak United States and very low US interest rates. I personally have doubts about yen sustainability.

Monitoring what has happened to European currencies against the dollar has been made trickier in the last twelve years by replacement of the deutschmark and other European currencies by the euro. Although the value of the euro has fluctuated more around its GSDEER-predicted path than the yen, its long-term performance has broadly been as expected. In this regard, all three of the major currencies –

the dollar, yen and euro – have in the broadest sense evolved in line with the model's fundamentals. The current monetary system has served this part of the world well.

Applying a similar model to the BRIC economies strongly suggests that the real equilibrium exchange rate for each will rise considerably against the dollar and other major currencies in coming decades. If the respective monetary authorities succeed in keeping inflation under control, this is likely to imply nominal appreciation in value. In the Goldman Sachs BRIC growth models, in fact, projected currency appreciation accounts for about a quarter of the potential US dollar value of GDP by 2050. Some of the projected future nominal GDP strength would not materialize if the BRIC currencies don't follow this anticipated path, but based on long-term history as well as events of recent years, it seems reasonable to assume that they will.

Getting to that point, however, is not so straightforward. For any country to grow while allowing its currency to float on the stormy seas of the foreign exchange markets is a nerve-wracking experience. In the so-called emerging economies, a whole variety of exchange rate systems has evolved, ranging from loose free floats for the Brazilian real and Korean won to heavily managed currencies such as the Chinese renminbi and Indian rupee. In Europe, of course, most of the continent's largest economies abandoned their own free-floating currencies to join the EMU. As the balance of world trade and the world's capital market developments change, it is difficult to see the world's monetary system remaining exactly as it is. What happens to both the value of and, more important, the use of the BRIC currencies is going to be a major issue.

Indeed, they will almost undoubtedly become part of the future global monetary system. Why? Well, consider again the possible path for the world economy in the current and next decade. Before the end of 2020, the BRIC economies combined will become larger than the US. Before the end of 2030, China may become as large as the US and the other BRIC economies may match those of the G7. Can we have a global monetary system that does not include the currencies of all of its biggest economies? No.

For the BRIC countries themselves, this is a vital domestic issue. If their policymakers want to ensure low and stable inflation, they will have to deal with the consequences of nominal exchange rate appreciation. Adopting a more flexible exchange rate system would be a useful tool in targeting inflation, which, as I have said, should be a priority for any ambitious developing economy. It would also help rectify the current balance of payments asymmetries, such as China's huge holdings of foreign exchange reserves. For years now, China has been on the other side of the United States' trade and current account deficits, sending out its exports and hoarding dollars and Treasury bills. The US has been putting pressure on China to let the renminbi appreciate in nominal terms. In 2010 and 2011, the Chinese did allow some modest nominal appreciation, but perhaps not quickly enough to offset the impact of the earlier stance, and as a result let some inflation into their economy. How China handles this classic struggle between managing its currency and managing inflation will define its relations with the world for years to come.

Brazil offers a very different model. In 1999 it introduced a formal target for inflation, in an attempt to end decades of hyperinflation and accompanying currency crashes. Since then, its economy has stabilized and grown, and its currency has become particularly popular with investors. This would have been inconceivable just a few years ago. The Brazilian real may well be on its way to becoming an important global currency.

The rise of the BRIC currencies might ultimately threaten the supremacy of the dollar as the currency of international trade, finance and exchange rate setting. It is apparent from the communiqués of BRIC finance ministers and leaders I read that an increasing amount of bilateral trade among the BRICs is bypassing the dollar and being conducted in their own currencies. As the BRICs continue to grow, and rival the US and G7 in size, this trend is bound to increase.

There will be similar, unpredictable, consequences in the rest of the world. The euro will be challenged by the rise of the BRIC currencies, assuming that it will survive its considerable current challenges. Except for China, none of the other BRIC countries is likely to approach the size of the US or the EU in the next twenty years. India and Russia, though, might match Italy, France, Germany or even Japan.

So, while it is inevitable that the currencies of Brazil, India and Russia will be more desirable for trade and investment, it is only in the unlikely event that the BRIC countries were to share a currency that their combined economic weight might be relevant in the monetary context. And I find it difficult to conceive of such a shared currency. The problems the European Monetary Union has been experiencing of late have only strengthened scepticism about the number of countries that use the euro. Using an external currency means ceding overall control of monetary policy, at the very least, and in hard times the acceptance of even tougher constraints on domestic fiscal and broader economic policies than would be necessary with a sovereign currency. Given their many differences, it is hard to see the BRICs making the concessions and commitments required to share a currency.

The renminbi alone has the potential to join the dollar and the euro as a global reserve currency. China is already close to being the largest exporter in the world. Even if over the coming decade its exports were to grow at half the 2000 to 2010 rate, China would still easily become the world's largest exporter. At the point when it is the world's largest economy and largest exporter, it is hard to imagine its currency not assuming an importance equal to the dollar and the euro. As China's capital markets develop, investors will clamour for more renminbi in order to hold more Chinese equity and debt. As I will discuss in the next chapter, by 2030 a neutral benchmark of global equities is going to have to include considerably more exposure to China and the other BRICs, which in turn will drive demand for the BRIC currencies.

We are already seeing the seeds of this trend being sown in Hong Kong, which the Chinese seem keen to develop as an offshore centre for the renminbi. Since mid-2010 the Chinese authorities have permitted greater use of the renminbi there and individuals have seized the opportunity to own the currency. Hong Kong also has a growing renminbi bond market. In February 2011, the World Bank issued its first renminbi bond. A number of international companies have done the same, with McDonald's being the first.

At some point in the future, China will probably make its currency fully convertible, insofar as it would be available for use by all Chinese citizens and the rest of us without any restriction. Many others would certainly like it to. Today, the

UK Treasury and other major governments, for example, cannot really hold any reserves of renminbi because it is not convertible. Many pension funds will not invest in China for the same reason. Once that changes, prodigious sums of international money could more easily flow into China.

There are of course risks to this and the Chinese and the other BRICs are right to be careful. They worry that traders will make their currencies volatile, and don't want to introduce free-floating exchange rates until their domestic financial markets are more fully developed. The Chinese know that the Americans don't care about Chinese currency convertibility for its own sake. The Americans want a stronger renminbi because it would strengthen US manufacturing. But perhaps the Americans should be careful what they wish for. If China's currency were to strengthen a great deal, America would no longer be able to blame China for its own economic weakness if its domestic industry failed to gain dramatically as a result of business returning to the (now relatively cheaper) US from (the now relatively more expensive) China. While the US will benefit from a rise in the renminbi, it is likely that other less well-advanced nations such as Mauritius and some among the N-11 – Bangladesh and even Mexico, for example – could benefit just as much, and so reduce the direct benefits for the US. I continue to believe that the rise of the Chinese consumer will be more important to the future health of the US than the value of the Chinese currency.

China has given quite a lot of thought to these monetary issues. Again, return to 1997 and the Asian currency crisis, when China showed it could identify the real problem (the weakness of the yen) and persuade America to do something about it. It showed an impressive degree of economic muscle and understanding. The Chinese might prefer a foreign exchange market that they can control, perhaps their own version of Bretton Woods. I do side with those who believe the world is better off with floating exchange rates and fewer currency controls, properly managed. But I am not doctrinaire about it.

There may be another future path the renminbi could take, an alternative to the free float and convertibility that many of us in the West assume are the only options. So far I have focused on the conventional view that as China's capital markets become more established and it relaxes controls on trade and currency movements, the renminbi will move inexorably into place as a free-floating, freely traded global currency. But in the past few months I have found myself starting to imagine a different, perhaps less conventional monetary future. It is conceivable that China could become as large as suggested but that the Chinese authorities do not allow a free float of the renminbi or free use of it across China's borders. It is conceivable that China, along with the other BRICs, might try to persuade the rest of us that a free-floating monetary system is not as useful as we all think, and a different monetary system could emerge.

Western economists tend to think that developing economies move along predetermined paths towards greater openness, and that global interconnectedness leads to greater stability. But increasingly I find myself wondering whether China and the other BRICs will be quite so eager to embrace the floating exchange rate system and allow their currencies to become more like reserve currencies. While the US and other developed countries such as the UK, Australia, Canada and the like still believe in the virtues of floating exchange rates, it is not clear that any of the BRIC countries share their enthusiasm.

Even the build-up to the introduction of the euro offers a precedent. While the US authorities have happily embraced the reserve-currency status of the dollar for a long time, not all Europeans, notably German policymakers, have been so keen on a similar fate for the euro. Being a reserve currency entails certain costs, notably increased demand which can seriously deplete the issuer's balance of payments. Certainly before the euro's existence, German policymakers were never keen on the Deutschmark playing such a role, which would have committed them to considering the external consequences of their domestic policy decisions.

This dilemma will become more acute for China's monetary mandarins as their economy gets bigger and more and more of us want to use their currency for trade and investment purposes. Chinese policymakers will, I'm sure, think long and hard about what they want to achieve by granting a greater global role to the renminbi.

When Chinese leaders talk about the importance of a new international currency system, they do not simply mean the elevation of their own currency to reserve status. In 2009 China's central bank governor, Zhou Xiaochuan, observed that 'the outbreak of the [financial] crisis and its spill-over to the entire world reflects the inherent vulnerabilities and the systemic risks in the international monetary system' and urged the world 'to create an international reserve currency that is disconnected from individual nations'. He mentioned the 'Triffin dilemma', identified by the economist Robert Triffin, who observed that in the fixed-rate Bretton Woods system, the supplier of a reserve currency will always end up running deficits in its balance of payments in order to keep up with demand for its currency. The United States keeps printing dollars and the Chinese and Japanese keep buying them.

In this context I also find myself wondering whether there might be a bigger role for the so-called Special Drawing Right (SDR), and for the BRIC currencies within it. This idea has become increasingly fashionable among policymakers and academics, and was suggested by the French when they chaired the G20 in 2011. Special Drawing Rights are claims to a basket of US dollars, sterling, euros and yen, allocated to countries by the IMF as an alternative to foreign exchange reserves. The SDR is not a true currency in the same way as the dollar or the euro: it is the IMF's accounting unit. Under IMF rules and usage, the component currencies of the SDR are changed every five years (most recently in 2010). They are determined by the proportional role played by that currency's country in exports, and by its use in foreign exchange reserves of central banks. The French have proposed that the basket should include the renminbi, although they were careful not to suggest a date. Given China's export prominence, the argument for its inclusion seems overwhelming. And based on the likely rise of China's share of global trade, its absence from the SDR will become odder and odder.

The argument for early inclusion is weakened, though, by the fact that the renminbi is not currently important as a currency for central bank reserve management. It is often believed that the IMF rules state that a currency needs to be freely convertible to be eligible for SDR involvement, because logic suggests that countries will not want to hold a currency within its reserves unless that currency is freely usable and convertible. But the French authorities, I suspect, believe that offering SDR membership to the renminbi might encourage China to accelerate the pace at which it makes its capital account convertible, as well as the pace of renminbi appreciation. Whether the Chinese would see the benefits of early participation of the renminbi in the SDR is debatable – especially if it were to impose on them a faster timetable for decisions about the use of the renminbi than otherwise.

But there are also significant arguments against expanding use of the SDR. If the purpose of bringing the renminbi into the SDR is to pry open China's monetary system, then once that system is open, why would investors want to hold the SDR? If they had access now to the renminbi as well as other highly liquid currencies, why bother with the SDR? One of the major reasons private investors do not hold much SDR today is that they can easily buy and sell its component currencies. An even more significant problem is that if you try to turn the SDR into a world currency, then you also have to create a World Central Bank to back it up. I find it hard to imagine the United States, or any other major economy, giving up control over domestic policy in order to be part of a world monetary system. It would take a bold politician even to suggest such a measure.

As for the Chinese, I also wonder if their interest in expanding the SDR arises as much from a desire to have complete control over their currency without succumbing to the external responsibilities imposed by having a fully convertible renminbi. It probably also stems from nervousness about the continued role of the dollar in the future. All in all, even if China is to become the world's largest economy and trading nation, I am not entirely convinced that its policymakers will allow the currency to be as liquid and tradable as the dollar.

One thing is for sure: if the world economy continues to unfold in the manner I expect, the monetary system is likely to evolve into something very different.

9

Invest and Prosper

It should be clear by now that I no longer regard the BRICs as emerging markets. They are a fundamental part of the modern world. If someone says they want to invest in BRICs because they want to invest in emerging markets, I ask them to leave the room. (And sometimes they don't realize that I'm joking.)

The BRICs can't be labelled 'emerging' in the same way as a traditional emerging market such as Ukraine or Venezuela. Yet I still run into this attitude all the time. I was recently talking to a US pension fund manager whose trustees would not let him invest in the BRICs as, supposedly, 'all these countries do is steal jobs'. He was asking me what he should do. 'Find a new job,' I told him, this time only half in jest. We all tend to stick with the behavioural styles we grew up with. But it seems ridiculous these days to keep thinking of the BRICs as emerging, and applying outdated risk metrics and forecasts to countries and companies which are quite different. At Goldman Sachs we came up with the Growth Markets concept to help people get out of this old way of thinking.

Talk to multinational companies such as JCB, Burberry, WPP or General Motors. Do they think of China as an emerging market, or as an essential part of their present and future?

It has been companies such as these rather than Western investors who have embraced this concept earliest and with the most confidence. They seem less bothered by the issues of governance and rules of doing business than many investors. Perhaps the timing of the BRIC acronym, just as the technology, internet and media stock market bubble burst in 2001, gave many corporate planners and CEOs a new focus when they were desperately searching for one. Ironically, the technology created by that era probably allowed them to explore some of these distant opportunities more easily.

I constantly need to adjust my perspective on the BRIC markets. I have a long-term, fundamental bias, which naturally tends to great optimism about the opportunities over the next few decades. But I also hold shorter-term views which vary enormously from country to country, company to company, investment to investment, and market to market – always driven by my perception of value. With the BRICs, as with any economic trend, there is always plenty of noise and colour to influence one's view of reality, and these have to be combined with value and the strength of the underlying story to assess whether it is a good time to invest or not.

The key is to pay attention to the evidence and keep your emotions at bay. Investing in BRICs is no different from investing anywhere else. You must consider liquidity, the clarity of your investment goal and mission, the likelihood of being repaid and, of course, valuation. While I believe in my long-term expectations for the BRICs, it is important to stay objective as the future and new evidence unfold.

It is easy to be carried away by the momentum of a business theme, and it often leads investors to push market valuations far from fair value. Whenever I have seen this happening and a particular instrument or market seems highly valued, then it has usually been the right time to disinvest, irrelevant of what the theme is. The BRICs are no different. Conversely, when an instrument or market seems cheap and if commentators and media review the theme poorly, it is often a good time to invest. In a world where the internet gives everyone equal access to information, finding valuation distortions requires a lot of hard work, experience and sometimes a hunch and some guesswork. The smart investor is able to perceive fair value, and then ride the momentum before getting out before the mood or theme changes. It's not an easy trick to pull off once, let alone repeatedly over a lifetime of investing.

My years of following the foreign exchange market taught me to be careful about sticking with a theme that supposedly may go on for ever. It has also taught me not to believe that investments can diverge too dramatically for too long from fair value. It has happened repeatedly in both the dollar and the yen, as well as in the relatively short life of the euro. For the euro, our GSDEER work suggests fair value against the dollar is around $1.20. When the euro is trading below 0.90 as it was briefly in 2000, and analysts are describing it as a 'toilet' currency – as one was quoted at the time – it is interesting to look the other way. Similarly, when it got to $1.60 a few years ago, and people said the dollar would decline for ever, it was also a good time to explore the downside case for the euro.

Although the BRICs are such a vast and overwhelming subject, the same rules and criteria apply. At any moment in time, has the market priced in all the likely good news or not? When it seems so obvious, there is probably something you are missing. In my thirty years in finance, I've realized that the day everything becomes crystal clear is probably the day we should stop investing in that idea: it could not get any better, or perhaps something new will appear. So as big as the BRIC theme might become, one has to stay objective and open to the idea that it could one day become redundant.

Having said that, I have little doubt that as the BRICs comprise ever more of the world's GDP, their capital markets will develop and the opportunities will multiply for domestic and foreign investors to participate in their growth. There will be changes in both the supply of investments in the BRIC economies and the demand for global investments as the investor class in these countries expands. We are likely to see more sophisticated equity and credit markets, as well as improved regulatory and legal frameworks for investors, assuming the political desire for economic growth persists.

The BRIC story is now developing far beyond the narrow world of investing. In April 2010 I was invited to attend the London opening of an exhibition of BRIC art at Phillips de Pury & Company's auction house. In his preface to the exhibition catalogue, the company's chairman, Simon de Pury, wrote: 'In the art world, like in the business world, decades of "westernization" are rapidly being replaced by an "easternization".' Given the astounding growth in India and China, you could say the same of investing.

In London, the wealth which has accrued to the BRIC elites is constantly on display. They buy football teams, the very best residential property, and art. The 'season' of social events which runs from late spring through the summer, including Wimbledon and the Chelsea Flower Show, now has a strong Indian and Russian presence. Brazilian and Chinese investors frequently pass through my office laden with shopping bags.

My own obsession, football, is increasingly intertwined with the BRIC world. The World Cup is to be hosted in 2014 in Brazil and in 2018 in Russia. The Olympics are following a similar pattern: 2008, Beijing, winter 2014, Sochi, 2016, Rio de Janeiro. India cannot be far behind. A number of academic institutions around the world have started generalist BRIC institutes and BRIC lecture series. I was invited to one of the universities in Rio de Janeiro in 2009. I am sure more invitations will follow.

Another illustration of the BRICs' rise is the annual listing in *Forbes* magazine of the world's dollar billionaires. At the start of 2011, the BRICs had 301 of the world's 1,210 billionaires, one more than Europe. This is about commensurate with the BRICs' share of global GDP. Between 2010 and 2011, the BRICs added 108 billionaires, a sign of their rapid growth. China alone had 115 and some believe that *Forbes* is underestimating the number of Chinese billionaires by half. A friend in Hong Kong reckons there are now more billionaires in China than in the United States. Her suspicion may become fact within a few years. The *Forbes* list is just another example of how multifaceted the story of the BRICs can be: disturbing from one angle, but irresistible from another.

Of course, the fact that the BRICs can have more billionaires than Europe with less GDP, and even less GDP per capita, suggests an unhealthy inequality in these countries. Much of the BRICs' new wealth is going into the pockets of a small group at the top of the economy.

History suggests this is not unusual. When countries experience rapid wealth increases, elites benefit the most. Sometimes when that rapid wealth accumulation slows, and especially if countries are beset by problems such as inflation or simple cyclical downturns, political and social problems multiply.

Social unrest and resentment towards these economic elites inevitably follow. To avoid this central banks will have to restrain inflation and support a broader sharing of wealth creation. This is one of the most important and necessary challenges lying ahead for the BRICs.

When I originally dreamt up the BRIC concept, the question of how investors could make the most of this economic theme seemed tougher to answer than today. New emerging markets had a troubled history for investors, and remember that this was soon after the bursting of the technology stock market bubble. Many investors didn't seem to think that the BRIC theme was one that mattered.

In fact, as noted earlier, multinational companies seized on the BRICs quicker than other Western investors. It was much easier to benefit from investing in the BRICs at a time when not so many were focused on it. Again, it pays not to be in the same camp as a 'lazy consensus' when it comes to investing.

I have often thought that business travel, difficult though it can be for personal relationships, is vital to understanding how the world changes, especially when it comes to the BRICs. Perhaps to those who don't travel very much, as well as those who have strong views on the appropriate form of political governance, the BRIC opportunity has always seemed much more risky than exciting. I still encounter many who are sceptical of all the BRICs' opportunities, the degree of scepticism varying according to the BRIC concerned and the form of investment on offer. There are also those who look at the rapid growth in BRIC economic activity and see a bubble waiting to burst. Perhaps the BRIC story will disappoint at some point in time? Perhaps it will become a major bubble? But perhaps, just perhaps, the 2050 dream scenario will come true. If so, it is a theme for tens of millions to embrace.

It is vital not to get emotional about the BRICs, but rather to consider them as clinically as one would any other investment opportunity. In each country there are public and private equity, fixed income, commodities and foreign exchange markets at various stages of development. Some are more liquid and accessible than others, some better regulated. But at a high level, my own view is that the BRICs are on a path to greater economic maturity. We are likely to see all of these markets develop, grow stronger and become much more accessible.

More sophisticated capital markets will allow these countries greater flexibility in how they fund and manage their growth, and to be better integrated into the global financial system. For their individual citizens, economic growth will lead to better investment, pension and insurance schemes, which in turn will create huge new pools of investable capital.

This money will transform the world's financial institutions. As the BRIC economies become larger, healthier and more influential, I believe the debate over whether or not to invest in them will become redundant. They will no longer be considered a special phenomenon. Investments involving the BRICs should become as commonplace as those in current developed markets like the US, UK and Japan. I hope I am still actively following the markets when that happens.

This is not to say that investing in the BRICs on a day-to-day or even year-to-year basis is straightforward. Given the rapid changes in the BRIC economies, the usual challenge of assessing future earnings and therefore accurate price–earnings ratios requires as much careful judgement, and maybe more, as other markets. Compared to the BRICs, it is still relatively easy to predict the growth of, say, the UK economy over a ten-year period. As the demographics don't change much and neither does productivity, the underlying trend is stable. Mature economies do not deviate much from their underlying trend over time. Trying to predict the exact trend growth of the BRIC economies is considerably harder, because we don't actually know with any certainty what their underlying trend growth rate is.

Central to my thesis, and to my confidence in it, is that their trend growth rates have improved, and in some cases will improve further in the future. But equally they might follow years of rapid growth and then suddenly experience a sharp, though hopefully temporary, slowdown. Russia is a really good example. Before 2007, Russia grew much more than we believed was sustainable. Many then assumed that the growth it was experiencing would simply continue uninterrupted. In 2008 we found that it didn't when growth slowed dramatically. Some now take the opposite view, believing that Russia won't really grow much at all in the future. This too is very unlikely. For Russia and the other BRICs and the N-11 economies, there will be cyclical variation around a trend.

To complicate matters, not all BRIC markets are equal, and certainly their local markets do not always perform in line with their predicted GDP growth rate. Between 2001 and 2010, China reported the strongest GDP growth of the BRICs, but had the least impressive stock-market performance. This causes many to think that China is not a good place to invest, especially in stocks and shares. While this is an important issue to understand, it has to be kept in some perspective. While China's markets have underperformed compared to the other BRICs in the past ten years, they have

massively outperformed their US and European counterparts.

Economists and investment strategists have long haggled
over whether GDP growth is a useful guide to equity market
performance. Swiss stocks have been among the most profitable over the past fifty years, easily outperforming the Morgan
Stanley Capital International (MSCI) Emerging Markets index
over the long term, despite modest GDP growth. Some say
this is evidence that emerging market equities will always
ultimately disappoint. I believe that this historical evidence is
irrelevant to the core thesis about the BRICs.

The recent past and, more importantly, the future for the
economies of Brazil, Russia, India and China, are something
quite new, a transformation in the global economy which
turns economic history on its head. If the BRIC dream comes
true, then the evidence of the past fifty years is not going to
be relevant. The whole concept is that these countries have
emerged into different nations. If so, then investment in their
national markets today will continue to give incredible
returns in the future, regardless of long-term history.

Our projections of growth up to 2050 spurred a dedicated
BRIC fund investment industry. Goldman Sachs Asset Management (GSAM) and several of its competitors around the
world introduced specialist BRIC equity funds. At least $20
billion has been invested.

The scope for BRIC investment markets to grow is still
huge. By 2030, the market capitalization of public companies
in emerging markets, including the BRICs, could overtake
that of developed markets, rising from $14 trillion in 2010 to
$37 trillion by 2020 and $80 trillion by 2030 – that's 31 per
cent to 44 per cent to 55 per cent of global equity capitalization. According to one set of Goldman Sachs estimates,

Chinese market capitalization may exceed that in the US by 2030. As this process gathers speed, savers in developed markets will be compelled to own more emerging-market equities in order to balance their portfolios. Since February 2011, GSAM has had an N-11 Fund too, and despite the challenging global environment, we witness a steady inflow of investment to it.

In September 2010 my colleagues Timothy Moe, Caesar Maasry and Richard Tang estimated that, by 2030, what are now considered emerging-market equities will comprise up to 18 per cent of Western investors' neutral portfolios. This will require net purchases of $4 trillion of equities.[1] Acquisitions on this scale and the incorporation of more BRIC and emerging-market equities in developed-market portfolios will reduce the volatility of these investor equity portfolios. There is a major opportunity here for financial institutions, but it will require an investment of business resources, and more localization.

There is still a great debate within the industry as to whether BRIC funds are anything more than a marketing theme. Some believe investors should stay well away from such theme-based approaches. In my new life as chairman of GSAM, I am learning that this is one of the great conceptual issues facing the asset management industry. Clients want good service, reliability and, of course, a good return. A theme-based investment fund might be a good way of raising assets but it will not necessarily give clients the experience they want, and it depends heavily on the success of the investment manager. The BRICs, I believe, are different: strong enough as a theme to make a highly sensible investment strategy. As the BRIC economic story continues to unfold, then the specialist BRIC investment fund industry is likely to grow much more across every asset class.

The 2010 paper by Moe et al. explained the significant shifts we can expect to see just in global equity markets over the next two decades. Their work influenced me as I moved to my current role at GSAM and I tried to devise ways to explain and measure what is going on in the BRICs for our investors.

A vital part of this process is to build a useful benchmark. The problem when dealing with a phenomenon as new and potent as the BRICs is which benchmark to use. I began by considering the relative merits of market capitalization and GDP-weighted benchmarks. My first instinct was that market cap benchmarks gave too much weight to previous company performance, and failed to take into account the startling changes in the BRIC economies. Market cap benchmarks, I felt, led investors into already highly capitalized and fully valued stocks. But the more I thought about this, I realized that GDP benchmarking would go too far in the opposite direction. As I have already noted, many multinationals from the developed world have experienced rapid earnings growth from the BRICs and other emerging markets. A GDP-weighted benchmark would not acknowledge this fact, and would probably end up overweighting BRIC exposure. Anyone investing solely on the basis of GDP growth forecasts would have missed the phenomenal decades-long rise in Swiss equities.

A smarter approach, then, would be somehow to combine the two. Coincidentally, as I was trying to work all this out, Goldman's quantitive research staff had been examining the volatility characteristics of investors' portfolios. The global credit crisis of 2007–8, the savage bear market in equities and the associated disruptions of many traditional investment beliefs compelled us to recognize that investors are much more interested in absolute returns than how their investments perform relative to a benchmark, as well as the volatility of a portfolio. In a collapsing market, comparing yourself to how others are doing, the essence of benchmarking, rather than concentrating on generating absolute, positive returns, can quickly leave you hungry and broke. As I have become fond of saying, 'Investors don't eat relative returns, they eat absolute ones.'

The Holy Grail for me became an approach which combines minimum volatility, to reassure investors in difficult times, with exposure to the revenue growth of quoted companies from around the world, regardless of their domicile. If you can achieve this, you could have a portfolio which avoids the most highly rated and capitalized stocks while offering more exposure to the Growth Markets. Such an approach, applying a neutral weight to individual countries, would be very different from most current approaches, which benchmark against the country-weighted MSCI.

Getting the benchmark right is more than a purely technical issue. Even within Goldman Sachs I have colleagues who worry that by leading the push to change benchmark behaviour, we could endanger our brand if the BRIC dream never materializes. I understand their caution but we all have to move with the times to maintain a brand and show leadership. Only time will tell whether the approach I am proposing influences people.

Benchmarks are just one of many issues that we need to make sense of in the blizzard of conflicting information which emanates from the world of investing.

On a broad economic basis, I believe that – contrary to the pessimistic mood which engulfed the West after the credit crisis and again in the summer of 2011 – the global economy is growing faster now than it ever has over the past thirty years. I try to show this for investors by focusing on the links between growth and asset returns. And I suggest that it is reflected in the equity risk premium (ERP), the extra return investors can expect on average for taking the risk of holding equities rather than so-called risk-free government bonds.

The trend of the world economy appears to be now growing a bit more than 4 per cent a year, versus 3.7 per cent over the past thirty years, because of the BRICs. If growth is a proxy for long-term earnings growth, then this means that company earnings around the world are rising faster than in the past. The ERP carries a lot of useful information for investing at any moment in time. When it is high compared to its own long-term history, it is likely to come back down in coming years. It can come back down through strong equity market performance and/or a rise in the risk-free rate (the yield on government bonds). When the ERP is low, as it was around the 2000–2 period, investors are not adequately protected and subsequently equities do poorly as the ERP rises. In addition to higher global earnings, the current ERP is high because of high dividend yields and, of course, rather low government bond yields.

The increase in the equity risk premium in recent years suggests to me that shares should rise in the coming years. It does not help to determine whether you should invest in Western companies with large BRIC exposure, such as Louis Vuitton or BMW, or directly in the BRICs themselves. For equity investors today, this is the hardest question.

*

In 2009, on the back of the global crisis, China expanded bank lending and credit considerably. This probably has involved some lending that won't generate returns. I'm not blind to the fact that in the last decade the Chinese government had already had to deal with its worsening bad-loan problem by recapitalizing the banks using its foreign exchange reserves. They might have to do this again. After all, why hold such huge reserves if you aren't going to use them for something? I am fully aware that the boom in China during these last ten years was helped by exports and massive growth in investment. This is highly unlikely to be repeated in the decade ahead and beyond. Indeed, it would be worrying if it were. China now needs to be led by consumption.

I find more reasons for optimism than pessimism about the commercial impact from China and the rest of the BRICs. When I talk to global companies, whether it's Unilever, Nestlé or even my colleagues at Goldman Sachs, the excitement about the BRICs and the Growth Markets is palpable. When Kraft bought Cadbury in 2010, the British press painted the acquisition as the loss of a British icon to an American giant. What that acquisition was really about was Cadbury's business in India. The UK market was not at the forefront of Kraft's thinking.

I've been talking to US car companies for a very long time, and they were always pretty suicidal about their industry. Not today. Since the whole BRIC theme started, they've become much more fun to spend time with. Growth has transformed their mood. It could even be said that these days General Motors is more a Chinese company than an American one.

There are some reasons to be cautious about investing in Chinese equities. Some of the publicly quoted companies might be companies without much quality and sustainably profitable business models. It can be dangerous for those eager to explore investors' fascination with all things China. I can understand those who prefer to invest in China by working with privately owned partnerships run by people who thoroughly understand China's domestic markets. I invest in some Chinese private businesses and in some private investment vehicles. Some public investments have also done rather well. Goldman Sachs' earnings have been helped by our investment in the publicly listed ICBC bank in recent years. Some of my own personal Chinese investments have been among my more successful ones. The CEOs of big global companies want to be confident that they can get a good return on their investments and, when they want, are able to get their money out of China.

Not surprisingly, some Chinese find it odd and contradictory that Western businesses can criticize their public markets when the West had its own financial crisis and the US had to deal with severe crises at, for example, Enron and Arthur Andersen, as well as across the financial services industry. Russians hear us fretting about investing in some of their companies and say the same thing. Lots of BRIC policymakers don't talk about a global credit crisis, but rather the North Atlantic credit crisis. What some of us see as natural investor anxiety, they see as prejudice. Beyond the usual justified paranoia of investing, at times it is tough not to have quite a bit of sympathy with their view.

When I listen to China's leaders describe their ambitions, I start to think that the issues we see today are really just those of any markets that are emerging. We see the United States and the United Kingdom constantly revising and updating their financial regulatory systems. No market is ever perfect and so one must look to what each country aspires to. China,

I believe, aspires to more open, transparent and liquid markets. It wants Shanghai to become a major world financial centre, especially for equities. It wants Western companies to list some of their stock there. HSBC bank is just one of the global companies to say that's a very real possibility. This would allow global companies to tap fresh capital by letting 1.3 billion people add their stock to their investment portfolios. The only reason companies aren't doing this already is because they are worried about the costs of doing so. What would it entail? What would be the regulatory consequences? What would be the impact on governance?

I would be staggered if by 2015 there weren't several major Western companies with at least some equity listed in Shanghai. The Chinese want it and I'm sure the Western companies could use the capital. For China's policymakers, the downside is that its equity markets could grow to the point where the slightest bump in them will panic global investors and make the economy more vulnerable to large capital outflows. The Chinese may become familiar with the phrase 'escalator up, elevator down'. Investors, whether domestic or foreign, arrive singly, but when things go wrong, they can quickly depart en masse. This can create enormous volatility and instability, two things the Chinese fear especially. But they also know this might be a price worth paying as they want to advance and have more foreign expertise helping them develop.

The development of China's markets in the coming years will be defined by the balance between two factors: the desire to open up and broaden these markets without allowing them to be capable of knocking China off its growth path.

The speed of local investment management development is also remarkable. As recently as 2007, when I went to Beijing to talk to Chinese investors I would primarily meet government officials at the State Development Bank, the People's Bank of China and SAFE, the State Administration of Foreign Exchange. These days, I meet private Chinese fund managers, and I talk with them as I would with hedge fund managers in London and New York. The speed at which they have learned, and the quality of their questions, is astounding.

There is no equivalent to the huge private Western fund managers yet in China, but they are emerging. Goldman Sachs has a good relationship with ICBC in China, and when I meet people in their distribution division, I am reminded of the similar investment giants from both the past and today in Japan. They built their business by going door to door to woo Japanese investors.

Many foreign companies find it more difficult to invest in India than in China. They see resistance from Indian policy-makers and find it difficult to deal with the sheer number of people it takes to get beyond the system. For Indian policy-makers, accepting a big foreign multinational can be a hard political sell. Indian politicians often seem to assume that any foreign investment will be interpreted as foreign exploitation. This can be very frustrating for international companies. India's financial system could be a tremendous investment opportunity today, if only one could get access to it. Indian household credit is 8 per cent of GDP, a sign of an economy functioning purely on cash. Any financial services firm that can help develop something closer to a Western retail banking system could probably make a lot of money as well as help India to transform. To get to where it could, India needs to outgrow some of these tendencies.

Ironically, and in contrast to many international companies, financial investors typically find India a lot easier to invest in than China, partly due to India's colonial history and perhaps its English-based legal system.

Every country, BRIC or not, has its investment quirks. In Russia, the main concern is also often the government. I know people who have made enormous sums trading the most liquid Russian energy stocks, such as Gazprom. But anyone tending to invest in anything sensitive to those in the Kremlin, and who makes a lot of noise about it, risks trouble. That said, the Russians today are talking seriously about creating a special centre for trading financial instruments in the ex-Soviet republics that make up the Commonwealth of Independent States.

Brazil is probably the easiest of the BRICs from an investing perspective. It is more Western and democratic than the others and has better established domestic capital markets. Goldman has a thriving securities business there, with quite significant interest rate and currency markets. It is GSAM's fifth most important market, and presently more developed than those in India and China. It is easily the most popular BRIC investment destination among private investors, including foreign and domestic private equity investors.

This means I worry a little. If everything seems so good, I like to worry. We all constantly have to weigh up risk, opportunity and what the consensus has already decided the value should be.

As I have mentioned, private equity is a very exciting area for BRIC investors. Part of the reason is the lack of free float in the market's public equity markets, as well as the possibility of forging links with local experts and experienced native thinkers and business people. Government entities still control large portions of public equity in the BRIC markets, either directly or indirectly, and place limits on foreign investors. Private equity offers a different range of opportunities. Shortly before the Blackstone Group – a leading investment and advisory firm – listed publicly in 2007, it sold 10 per cent of its shares to China's sovereign wealth fund, the CIC. It was a smart move by Blackstone for several reasons: not only did it give the company an important seal of official approval as it sought out investments in China, it also allowed the Chinese to invest money overseas through Blackstone funds without attracting the many raised eyebrows that seem often to accompany major sovereign wealth investments.

These days, many private equity firms are rightly looking at all kinds of opportunities in China, notably high-potential consumer plays. There are more and more Westerners who have set themselves up in China to do just this kind of investing.

Russia is a country where different firms take very distinct positions. Many, including some of the sharpest, toughest, best-connected private equity firms in the world, appear much less inclined to do business there. Yet others, such as the Texas Pacific Group, seem to have no psychological barriers to investing there. Interestingly, very recently, a number of experienced global investors appear to have made a much bigger commitment to Russia and are committed to an exciting new fund, half of which will consist of Russian government capital.

As I have pointed out, India can sometimes feel like a prohibitive place for many investors, often offering tantalizing returns, yet frustrating prospects as it is difficult to get things done. Companies investing there can become entangled in bureaucracy, poorly drafted regulations and corruption cases. The Indian press and political class jump eagerly on even the slightest hint of corruption, especially when it involves foreign companies. Ambiguous tax laws for foreign investors exacerbate the challenge. In 2007, Vodafone acquired a stake in the Indian mobile operator Hutchison Essar, and has spent the years since battling through the courts over the taxes owed on the deal.

Opportunity has to be weighed against risk. Vodafone has also invested $23 billion in India in anticipation of a large, long-term opportunity. Big deals can get done in India, but it takes extraordinary patience. This explains partly why foreign direct investment in India has been weaker than in the other BRICs. The government makes it difficult even in areas where they, in theory, allow it. If India had a friendlier environment for foreign investors, foreign direct investment would grow sharply.

Over time, the development of local fixed income markets in the BRICs will be even more exciting. Today the credit markets in China and India are in their infancy. Their bond markets are small, consumers save rather than borrow, and companies depend on bank lending or informal cash transactions to fund their growth. Despite enormous infrastructure needs, the system of credit to fund roads, railways and airports remains primitive. On the demand side, investors are frustrated by the lack of investment opportunities. As the BRICs develop mutual funds and pension and insurance pools, there will be ever larger blocs of capital to be deployed. The history of economic development tells us that with economic growth comes the development of credit markets.

In the early 1970s the G7 bond markets were roughly similar to those of China today. What transformed them was financial deregulation, such as abolition of interest rate and foreign exchange controls, the liberalization of fees and commissions, and finally demographics. As countries become more economically mature, their population ages, pension and life insurance markets develop, increasing the demand for bonds, and government lending rises due to lower tax revenues and greater provisions for health care and social security. Economic development consistently leads to a reduction in state ownership of corporations and control of the banking sector, which in turn leads to more evolved capital markets.

Between 1970 and 1995 the bond markets of Europe and Japan increased on average by the equivalent of 70 per cent of GDP. Our analyses show that just over two-thirds of that growth can be attributed to the expansion in income per capita. The richer a country becomes, the more it borrows. At Goldman Sachs we believe that, by 2016, Chinese bond market capitalization could rise to around $4.5 trillion in today's prices, about equal to the current size of the US Treasury market or as much as the German and French bond markets combined. This process of debt market expansion is likely to occur in all the BRICs and Growth Markets.

It is worth looking even more closely at the capital markets in the two largest BRICs, China and India. In China, there is a wide gap between its economic growth and the maturing of its capital markets. The debt markets are still dominated by government debt, or securities issued by its 'policy banks'. The fast-growing small and medium-sized enterprises have issued almost no debt, and have no bond market, despite comprising 60 per cent of GDP and generating 50 per cent of tax revenues. Instead, they must rely on retained earnings, bank loans and informal private financing, notably from Hong Kong and Taiwan. Greater access to formal debt markets would enable them to grow even faster. Their corporate bonds would also provide an excellent alternative investment for China's savers, whose funds languish in low-yielding bank deposits.

There are many advantages to a country in having a flourishing and vibrant debt market. It allows the more efficient allocation of resources across sectors and time. It means savers and institutions can invest rather than save. And it will allow the financing and sustaining of China's economic boom. If China continues to grow, as I believe it will, its debt markets will soon be an important part of the global economy.[2] The Chinese authorities still too often treat lending as an extension of government policy, allocating capital to achieve policy objectives in line with its priorities. The government has also made such extensive use of quantity and price controls to prevent economic overheating that it is tough for a market-oriented debt market to flourish.

The government's attitude is understandably shaped by what occurred in the 1980s and early 1990s, when weak institutions and a poor understanding of market mechanisms led to the collapse of China's fledgling corporate debt market. Today, we are seeing rapid changes and it is likely that China's debt capital markets will quickly catch up with the rest of its economic growth. In 2005 the People's Bank of China established a commercial paper market to try to jump-start corporate debt borrowing, and while volumes are still light, it is gaining speed. The Chinese authorities are experimenting in Hong Kong with so-called 'Panda Bonds', issued by foreign companies to raise money for investment back in China. As mentioned, McDonald's was the first to issue a renminbi bond to fund its growth in China, and there have since been several others. China is not yet channelling its domestic savings into the capital markets, but as its pension, insurance and mutual fund infrastructure develops, that will have to change.

Many of the same points could be made about India.[3] By 2016, the Indian debt market, public and non-public, could reach $1.5 trillion, two-thirds the size of Germany's debt market today. Indian development has already led to lower inflation, improved public finances and higher foreign direct investment and foreign currency reserves. Collectively, these have reduced India's vulnerability to shocks. But there remain serious concerns, notably the lack of transparency around its capital markets. So much Indian lending is done privately, which makes it next to impossible for public debt markets to develop. And yet the need for them is immense. More than any other BRIC, India is in dire need of developing its infrastructure. Indian corporate debt will be vital to this, and given its duration and link to inflation, such bonds would be attractive to pension funds and insurers the world over.

Like China, India needs to decouple its debt markets from its broader economic goals. It needs to stop ordering its institutional investors to hold lots of public sector securities as this distorts the market for them. At the moment, India is caught in a familiar bind, known to economists as the 'impossible trinity'. As it liberalizes the inflows and outflows of capital, it has to cede control of either its exchange rate or its monetary policy. If it tries to use interest rates to fix the value of its currency, in order to maintain its competitiveness, it risks capital pouring in and out to take advantage of the interest rate differential between India and its trading partners. If it tries to maintain the value of its currency by other means, such as buying it on the open market, it risks a liquidity crunch. On the other hand, if it tries to restrict the rise in the value of its currency by printing more money, it risks inflation. The only way out of the impossible trinity is to liberalize capital markets, so that over time interest rates converge with international rates, and there is less chance of being held hostage by foreign investors and their hot money.

There are also plenty of regulatory and technical changes India could usefully make. It could lower the high disclosure requirements it has for companies trying to issue bonds. Or reduce the high stamp duty rates on corporate debt. It could improve the legal framework for contract enforcement and lift the restrictions on foreign investors holding Indian corporate debt. It needs to encourage the emergence of market makers, develop better settlement and clearing systems and generally upgrade the environment for asset-backed securities. That way its capital account can finally become convertible, thereby allowing India its proper place among the world's economic giants.

While macro hedge fund investing involving the BRICs is pretty well developed, so-called long/short equity investing in the BRICs is relatively modest. The main problem is that the availability and diversity of stocks to short-sell are much less than in developed markets. Therefore, such funds cannot act with the same speed and efficiency they can in Western markets. As yet, the BRIC equity markets are simply not big or liquid enough and the ability to short stocks much more difficult than in the more advanced markets. If you believe that Chinese banks are overvalued, for example, it is hard to find ways to short-sell them on any scale.

It is also probably true that the regulatory systems are also not as easy to deal with as they are in the West. That is changing, as investors find ways of coping with them and, more importantly, as BRIC markets develop and local regulators become more advanced, and want to help develop their local markets. More hedge funds are opening and hiring in Hong Kong, Mumbai and Singapore. Brazil, again, may be the most advanced in this regard. Arminio Fraga, the Brazilian central bank chief who developed his country's inflation-targeting policy, has had his own hedge fund for many years which included both a long/short business and a private equity arm. In India there are a growing number of hedge funds run by Indians who have returned home after cutting their teeth in New York or London.

The world of BRIC investment, then, is becoming extremely varied, with myriad perspectives and opinions. I was recently in Tokyo, where I met the head of a major retail bank, Resona, who told me that he had guided 13 million retail customers in and out of trading the Brazilian real, because of its yield. Historically there was no more conservative investor in the world than the Japanese retail investor, so their decision to trade in Brazil's currency is a great vote of confidence. At GSAM, we are now in the process of offering a Growth Market equity-based fund to be distributed by a third party in Japan.

Not far from my London office is the headquarters of Foster & Partners, the architectural practice responsible for some of the developing world's most dramatic new airports and skyscrapers. I occasionally go to see them and we discuss their role at the centre of BRIC urbanization. Until the global financial crisis, they were the biggest employers in the London borough of Wandsworth, and yet 85 per cent of their business had nothing to do with the UK. This brings me to the final essential part of BRIC investing: developed-market companies which are profiting from BRIC growth.

I'm seeing this pattern more and more, of Western companies growing more quickly than ever courtesy of the BRICs. If General Electric could get rid of its consumer financial arm and focus exclusively on manufacturing, heavy industry and infrastructure, it would probably be one of the best BRIC stocks in existence. General Motors, as I've noted, is as much a BRIC company as an American one these days. All the commodity companies are great BRIC investments.

I know some very smart people around the world who tell me that the best way to play the growth of China and India is to just trade the Australian dollar. I'm not sure I agree, but if you look back you can see how dramatically Australia's trading relationships have changed. Australia used to be regarded as a good lead indicator of the economic fate of the United States. Not any more. Its largest export partners, in order of size, are now China, Japan, Korea, India and then the United States. These days, Australia is looking ever more to the rapid growth in Indonesia, which is just three hours away from its west coast.

Australia will be in an incredible position for years to come, as it is rich in commodities and surrounded by fast-growing economies. The top end of the Sydney property market is already dominated by Chinese money, and I anticipate that becoming ever more true.

You could make a similar case for Canada and even Germany. I sometimes think of Germany as a fully developed way of investing in the BRIC theme. On my visits to Munich, when I go to companies like BMW and Siemens, I realize that China is more important to them than Germany or even Europe. Up in Hamburg, the once ailing port area has been completely regenerated thanks to trade with Asia.

Britain has aspirations to become a leading partner of the BRICs. One of David Cameron's first overseas trips as prime minister was to Turkey, which he called the BRIC on our borders, and then on to India. London can often seem like the

BRIC capital of the world. Its convenient time zone, the dramatic rise of the English language and the UK's general open stance to foreign business and wealthy individuals has made London hugely attractive to many from the BRIC nations.

Britain is right to want to get more involved in BRIC growth, but its leaders have to do a better job understanding the BRICs and earning their trust. British service companies have great opportunities in the BRICs, in areas such as education, accounting and legal services. If Britain wants to succeed in creating stronger economic ties with these countries, its leaders will have to adjust their approach and not spend too much time trying to persuade them how to run their lives: accept them for what they are. For British companies to take advantage of new markets in the BRICs, their political leaders will have to be more thoughtful in their approaches.

The sheer range and number of global companies set to benefit from the growth in the BRICs prompted me and my old colleagues in investment research to create a developed BRIC Nifty Fifty index, through which investors can get BRIC exposure without having to invest directly in these markets. Since its inception a few years ago, this BRIC Nifty Fifty has strongly outperformed the MSCI Global index. We also created a separate Nifty Fifty for the BRIC countries themselves. By comparing the valuation of the two baskets at any moment in time, investors can choose whether it is more attractive to be involved in the developed market companies with BRIC exposure or directly in the BRIC markets themselves. Not surprisingly many investors watch the movements quite closely.

Of course, Goldman Sachs isn't the only bank to have understood the staggering opportunity. Many other institutions

and investors now grasp the potential in the BRIC economies. They realize what an important role the BRICs must
play in our everyday business decision making. One cannot
invest around the world these days and ignore or be frightened by the rise of the BRICs and the Growth Markets. It is
much better to be open-minded. Despite the instability such
changes bring, for millions of people around the world economic growth on this scale is a very positive story – and one
that can be good for our investments.

Conclusion: A Better World

The first ten years of my post-BRIC life have been a composite of study, analysis, remarkable travels and an inquiring intellectual journey around our world. Perhaps I can sense a glimmer of how it felt for the early pioneers and explorers. I am in the middle of an exciting and very different course for our century, in my own field of global macroeconomics.

The first decade of this journey has revealed to me a story that is emerging and developing beyond my highest expectations. That journey has transformed my thinking – from my early forays into considering the potential for the four BRIC nations to today's Growth Market world. The exciting prospects of these countries are good not just for them, but for us all. As we go through dramatic changes in the economic landscape it is important for people to keep remembering this.

The anecdotes that I have recounted in earlier chapters will multiply: Indians paying high prices to go up in ski lifts in Switzerland in the summer; Chinese traders offering rewards to native Parisians to buy them Louis Vuitton bags; Tibetan street traders walking across high mountain ranges in the Himalayas using mobile telephones; and Russian entrepreneurs developing some of the best global internet businesses. Such stories will grow and grow.

In July 2011, in the middle of the mayhem of the sovereign debt crisis raging in Europe and the US, one of the biggest news items that caught my attention was the earnings results from Apple. Revenues at the hi-tech gadget darling had risen sixfold in the first three quarters of 2010–11.

As desirable and must-have as Apple's iPhones and iPads are in the West, their second-quarter earnings were much stronger than expected owing to their sales in China. Like many other traded consumer companies, Apple are opening more outlets in Shanghai and other rapidly expanding wealthy Chinese cities. I've heard that one of the Shanghai stores attracts even more visitors than their famous glass cube on Fifth Avenue in New York. Just after the results were published, it was reported that some fake Chinese Apple stores were popping up – pictures of a shop in Kunming, a city in the south-west, were shown in the *New York Times*. Who said that the US can't benefit from the growth of the BRIC world? I wonder whether Apple's top executives still refer to China and those other nations driving world business as emerging, or whether they are joining the leadership at General Electric, who also now refer to them as Growth Markets?

For the over-indebted, burdened nations of the West, selling goods to the rising Growth Markets *is* their future. Before this decade is over, I expect the dollar value of consumption in the BRIC economies to exceed that of the US. Many of us in business and finance have grown up thinking that the US consumer drives the world. By 2020, this notion will be a mere historical observation. The next decade will power the BRIC economies to be bigger than the US, power the eight Growth Market nations to be nearly as big as the G7, and determine most Western multinationals' global success or failure.

In the early, rocky years following the global credit crunch it might seem to many in Europe and the US that the Western economic model is broken, that life will never be the same again, and that the BRICs are taking over at our expense. But my guess is that within a couple of years this depressing mood will lift. If the BRICs and N-11 achieve their goals it will be good for the world, and good for us.

In fact, the financial crisis gave my colleagues and me the chance to check on the robustness of our BRIC and N-11 assumptions. We found that collectively these fifteen nations have emerged from the crisis in much better shape than the major Western economies. While most of the G7 economies have not seen their output return to pre-crisis levels, virtually all the BRIC and N-11 countries recovered any lost output quickly and easily. In fact, three years on from the crisis, it seems the shift in the balance of world growth leadership has been accelerated, rather than hindered. This is a huge opportunity for the exporting sector of the developed economies, and presents the strongest opportunity for those economies most challenged to rebalance and restore health.

I passionately believe that if we stop thinking about these rising economic giants as purely exotic emerging markets, it might help us to understand better the balance of risks and opportunities. And this is why I call the BRIC nations, plus Indonesia, South Korea, Mexico and Turkey, Growth Markets. It is not a marketing gimmick or a way to sell a new investment fund. It is a way to help all of us think more globally.

Some of the rest of the N-11 countries might also enjoy this status in the future: Egypt, Nigeria, and even the Philippines. Those nations seem risky, mysterious, and possibly too unpredictable for many investors right now. But for them to reach their dreams of economic success would be fantastic for us all. Just imagine how transformational a large and wealthy Nigeria could be for the whole of Africa.

It might be that changes in the investing world could help others beyond it. I'm so excited each time Indonesian and Nigerian policymakers ask me about Goldman's latest growth environment scores. If we can help them to use such information to enable their vibrant populations to become wealthier then I would be proud. Actually, the fiscal health of most of the Growth Market economies is an additional force: investors can help develop a virtuous circle that could reward those nations that are successfully improving their act.

As I watched the scary sovereign debt crisis swirl in the summer of 2011, I found myself reflecting on the original Maastricht Treaty, which governed the criteria for countries joining the European Monetary Union. The Maastricht Treaty was signed ahead of EMU to ensure old-fashioned Bundesbank-style economic and financial discipline for all members. It stipulated no member's inflation rate should exceed that of the member with the lowest rate by more than 2 per cent, that budget deficits should not exceed 3 per cent or overall debt to GDP ratios 60 per cent (or at least be heading that way). Based on data for the actual fiscal and debt positions as things stand at the summer of 2011, only Finland of the current EMU members satisfies those criteria. Even Germany, fond of criticizing the other strugglers, doesn't quite make it on a rigid definition. In the unlikely event that other major developed nations should be judged on the same criteria, only Australia and Sweden and perhaps Canada come close. EMU could be technically feasible for these four countries. The UK, the US and, of course, Japan have an even worse debt position than the euro area average.

By contrast, most if not all of the Growth Market economies could satisfy the fiscal aspects of the Maastricht criteria, and all eight of them easily in terms of debt. Why then do we insist on calling them emerging markets? Their fiscal discipline is something that would make not only the German Bundesbank, but also perhaps the old-style Swiss central bank proud. If you add this fiscal responsibility to their remarkable growth potential, I really think it seems very outdated to think of those countries as emerging. Bringing some of their currencies into the IMF's currency basket, the SDR, and credible index creators such as Morgan Stanley and Standard & Poor's, can probably help many (not just investors) think differently about these nations.

I also passionately believe that one basic trend of international economic theory holds true: overall, international trade is good for everyone. Yes there are some losers, especially during the most challenging times of rapid adjustments, but not only theory but also evidence shows time and time again that we all benefit. Tens of millions of US consumers benefited for years from the success of Walmart bringing to their customers dramatically cheaper consumer goods, which was largely due to their success in importing products from China. As time has passed and China raises the incomes, wages and wealth of its citizens, it is not so easy for Walmart to employ this same tactic. It has to move on, and it is. Today, in addition to trying to keep itself at the forefront of supplying its domestic market with cheap affordable goods, Walmart is trying to expand significantly in the BRICs and beyond, with Brazil and South Africa as notable markets. This is similarly true for the UK's leading retailer, Tesco.

Anyone who struggles to see the trade benefits of the BRICs story should spend some time with the executives of BMW, Bosch, Mercedes, Siemens and countless other

German companies. Or perhaps the German trade statisticians. The chart showing the changing pattern of German exports since 2007 reproduced on page 116 is probably the most powerful single image I can think of depicting the scale of the change and opportunity facing us all. Today it is German exports, tomorrow it could be the UK and/or US. And not only in products. The *China Daily* recently carried an article about the setting up of a campus of Nottingham University in mainland China. The expansion of educational products and services could and should become a huge export opportunity for the West in both China and India.

The 2008 global credit crisis was the most frightening shock to me in my long financial career. We skirted perilously close to a prolonged and severe global economic slump, but our policymakers rescued us with bold and decisive action. The sluggish recovery in much of the West and rising unemployment are the remaining scars of that event, but I do find myself thinking that aspects of the crisis were not all bad. Raising the domestic US savings rate, reducing the US dependency on foreign capital and making others realize that they can't depend on the US consumer have to be positive developments.

Before its dramatic appearance and the crashing of the US housing market many, myself included, worried about the lack of a domestic household savings culture in the US, the country's seemingly never-endingly deteriorating external balance of payments, and (on the flip side) China's colossal export dependency on the US. This has all changed. The US is learning to save, it requires less foreign capital, its trade balance has improved slightly, and China certainly is trying to move away from an export model.

There are those who worry that the US is heading for fresh

trouble, especially when China stops buying so many US Treasury bonds, but this fear is overblown. It is only an outward sign of the worry that preoccupies the minds of the pessimists. If the US increases its domestic savings rate, which has gone from 0.6 per cent of income to around 5 per cent since late 2008, it means that the US will need less overseas finance. To improve imports, the US requires less foreign capital. In aggregate, the balance of payments will always equal zero; if the trade deficit declines, the capital inflow surplus will decline. The US should indeed welcome less Chinese (and other) foreign buying of US Treasuries, so long as its trade balance improves.

Despite all this, I can understand people's anxiety. Change, especially for those with narrow or manual skills, is always demanding. It might often seem that things will never be the same again. When I was growing up in Manchester in the 1960s and 1970s, that city was often portrayed as never being able to recover from the loss of the cotton industry. The same was said about Leeds and its wool industry, as well as of Liverpool and Newcastle with their dependency on the sea and on shipbuilding. Each of those cities still faces a variety of challenges, but life has moved on dramatically and in many ways they are thriving. Until the UK property market bubble burst in 2008, Leeds had arguably become the most buoyant major city outside London, a far cry from its historical roots. Even though Leeds has suffered in the fall-out from the credit crunch, I am hopeful that something fresh will appear as that city finds its edge.

The world's motor manufacturing industry often gets a lot of attention in the context of broader economic change, and it's true to say that its fortunes are highly illustrative of the BRIC story. While the UK no longer has its own domestic industry, lots of foreign companies produce cars in Britain.

When I travelled to meet clients and policymakers in Tokyo in June 2011, they told me that they thought the disruption to the supply chain from the tragic earthquake and tsunami in northern Japan would be felt all over the world; for instance a Japanese company, Renesas, produces 40 per cent of the world motor industry's hi-tech chips. Another policymaker predicted that the UK would probably see the largest negative consequences of the post-quake disruption. Sure enough, when the UK Office for National Statistics came to explain the UK's disappointing 0.2 per cent rise in real GDP in the second quarter of 2011, it cited the Japanese supply disruptions as one element hampering UK growth. The UK has some of the most productive plants of Honda, Nissan and Toyota.

Earlier in the book I gave several examples of how Germany sees direct benefits from the BRIC consumer appetite for its cars. BMW, Mercedes, Audi and VW all are experiencing dramatic growth in their sales to the BRICs, especially China. This destroys any myth that it is impossible for developed countries to maintain significant production and jobs in their own car industries.

This is something that US policymakers should ponder. Why is it that Germany, not a low-income country, can provide cars that the Chinese and Russians want to buy? Why is it that GM can only do the same by effectively turning itself into a Chinese company? It used to be said that what is good for General Motors is good for America. Maybe that is still true, and bodes well for the future of that company. If GM and Ford and Chrysler can produce what the rising wealthy Growth Markets' consumers want to drive, then it will.

In 2009, I participated in a fascinating debate with, among others, Larry Summers, then director of Barack Obama's US

National Economic Council. Larry kept talking about how, under the Democrat administration, life would be geared towards helping Joe from Flint, Michigan (the home of General Motors), and he inferred that policies might have to be introduced to influence world trade in order to achieve this goal. While I shared the implied view that the US would need to produce more at home, and export more to recover from the impending credit crisis, I took exception to the notion that world trade should be interfered with to simply help American auto workers.

I provoked Larry into debate by suggesting that he might not personally be that familiar with many 'Joes from Flint, Michigan', but I was, because I grew up in a region where manufacturing industries had become obsolete. I cited the regenerated plants in northern England (Derby and Sunderland), where the Japanese now produce cars. If US multinationals are to produce more manufacturing goods at home to satisfy foreign demand, then the right thing is for them to have the competitiveness and brand. German auto companies are demonstrating how it is done.

Of course, Larry is one of the smartest thinkers around, and he might be right. I appeared to be among the minority who believed President Obama's goal to double exports over five years from early in 2010 was actually achievable, because of the demand in the BRICs and Growth Markets. I still do, despite the Boston Consulting Group's recent prediction that within five years the US will recover any lost manufacturing competitiveness to China.

This is an exciting story. It goes far beyond business and economics. We are in the early years of what is probably one of the biggest ever shifts of wealth and income disparity in history.

It irritates me when I hear and read endless distorted stories of how only a few benefit and increase their wealth from the fruits of globalization, to the detriment of the marginalized masses. Globalization may widen inequality within certain national borders, but on a global basis it has been a huge force for good, narrowing inequality among people on an unprecedented scale.

Tens of millions of people from the BRICs and beyond are being taken out of poverty by the growth of their economies. While it is easy to focus on the fact that China has created so many billionaires, it should not be forgotten that in the past fifteen or so years, 300 million or more Chinese have been lifted out of poverty. In India the lives of many tens of millions have been similarly improved, and perhaps 300 million or more will join them in the next decade or two. Brazil has seen many millions of its population join its middle class and I have seen with my own eyes how one of their biggest favelas in Rio is now escaping destitution. Brazil has actually reduced its GINI coefficient, a widely used measure of inequality, indicating that the gap between its rich and poor is narrowing. We at GS estimate that 2 billion people are going to be brought into the global middle class between now and 2030 as the BRIC and N-11 economies develop. The same is beginning to happen in some of the most challenging parts of Africa, and while it is very early days, the uprisings in the Middle East suggest that it could happen there too.

Rather than be worried by such developments, we should be both encouraged and hopeful. Vast swathes of mankind are having their chance to enjoy some of the fruits of wealth creation.

This is the big story.

*

I want to finish with a specific example that reinforces this point. Tales of corruption, inefficiency and waste in India are all too familiar, and yet here is just one of the many initiatives being implemented to bring about monumental change.

In mid-July 2011 I was visited by an inspiring man from Delhi, a senior figure for the Unique Identification Authority of India (UIDAI). The UIDAI initiative was created by the Planning Commission in 2010 to provide all of the country's 1.2 billion people with their own unique twelve-digit identity, a process that will bring them into the welfare services, allowing even those living in the most remote parts of India access to health care, education and banking facilities for the first time. The head of the software giant Infosys, one of India's largest IT companies, has been seconded to implement the project.

The success of UIDAI would change the lives of hundreds of millions of Indians and their country. It could be genuinely transformational. It could also help in drastically reducing the role of the corrupt middlemen and getting rid of so much waste in the allocation of public resources by directly linking provider and consumer. The UIDAI people hope to be rolling out to 600 million Indians by 2014.

As he spoke, I found myself overcome with excitement for this project. If it is successful, then India may be a step closer to realizing the 'dream' of economic growth which they have embraced from our own mere projections. This very singular but remarkable example typifies what the BRIC story has done for me. And what I hope it will do for all of you.

Acknowledgements

I would never have created the BRICs concept, nor written this book, if it had not been for the wonderful opportunity of education. For that, I would like to thank my parents, who were determined that my three sisters and I would benefit from a good one.

I would also like to acknowledge those who encouraged me to pursue a career in finance and the many colleagues and friends I have met over the last thirty years in my professional life. To Professor Jim Ford, or at least he was in my day, at Sheffield for being imaginative enough to recommend me for a PhD at Surrey, without which I doubt I would have ever really progressed as an economist. Along with my dad, he seemed to be the only person who thought I was capable of attaining one.

Early in my career, it was my foreign exchange pals who taught me some of the most important realities about economics and financial markets and I am still indebted to them for that critical learning.

I remain grateful for the continued support of my colleagues at Goldman Sachs, many of whom have inspired and influenced me over the years. I should say a special thanks to Jon Corzine, Gavyn Davies, Steve Einhorn and Richard Witten, and especially to Lloyd Blankfein, all of whom were key in persuading me to join the firm in 1995. And thanks to David May, who in 2005 was the first to suggest I write a book on the BRICs.

Without Dominic Wilson and Roopa Purushothaman I am not sure that I would be in the position I am now. I am indebted to them for their seminal 2003 paper 'Dreaming with BRICs: The Path to 2050', which, I believe, really put BRICs on the map. Of course, I should say the same more broadly for all the wonderfully talented people I have had the pleasure of working with in the Global Economics department at Goldman Sachs. I must also say a special thank you to the rest of the BRIC 'alumni', including Swarnali Ahmed, Stacy Carlson, Themistoklis Fiotakis, David Heacock, Alex Kelston, Sandra Lawson, Raluca Dragusanu and now James Wrisdale, all of whom have helped some of the key BRIC stories along. Anna Stupnytska, who came over to GSAM with me when I joined as chairman in 2010, is more knowledgeable about all of the BRICs work than most of us, since she has been closely involved for much of the first ten years. She has been, and remains, key to many of my thoughts on the topic.

I must also say thanks to Linda Britten, the chief operating officer of the Economics, Commodities and Strategy Group, for being simply LB, Hannah Gower, my previous PA, and, of course, the wonderful Dawn Baker, who, in addition to typing several manuscripts, somehow manages to keep my life just about in order.

Thanks, too, to the various key people involved with the technicalities of the book, to Trevor Horwood for his copy-editing and to Joel Rickett and Adrian Zackheim of Penguin for taking the project on board.

I must also acknowledge many people in my relatively new life at GSAM, in particular Ed Forst and Tim O'Neill for persuading me to join, and Suzanne Escousse for all her support on this project as well as for the many weekends she has had to give up to edit my Viewpoints.

And lastly, let me say thanks to my two great kids, and to my wonderful wife, who has had to put up with this on top of everything else, for being my partner for the past thirty-two years.

Jim O'Neill

The author's advance in full, together with all royalties earned from the sale of this book, will be donated to the charity SHINE.

SHINE⋆

⋆**SUPPORT AND HELP IN EDUCATION**

SHINE: Support and Help in Education was founded in March 1999. Its mission is to support additional educational initiatives which encourage children and young people to raise their achievement levels. The charity funds organizations working with underachieving 6–18-year-olds from disadvantaged areas in London and Manchester. For more information please visit www.shinetrust.org.uk.

Notes

Introduction: Audacious Growth

1. Jim O'Neill, 'Building Better Global Economic BRICs', Goldman Sachs Global Economics Paper No. 66, November 2001.
2. Dominic Wilson and Roopa Purushothaman, 'Dreaming with BRICs: The Path to 2050', Goldman Sachs Global Economics Paper No. 99, October 2003.
3. Jim O'Neill, Dominic Wilson, Roopa Purushothaman and Anna Stupnytska, 'How Solid are the BRICs?', Goldman Sachs Global Economics Paper No. 134, December 2005.

1 The Birth of the BRICs

1. The Group of Five, or G5, was an informal grouping formed in the wake of the 1973 oil crisis, comprising the finance ministers of the five nations with the highest GDP per capita: the United States, Japan, France, West Germany and the United Kingdom. Italy joined in 1975, when the group was formalized as the G6, becoming the G7 a year later with the addition of Canada. Russian membership in 1997 expanded the group to its present G8 format.
2. The individual G20 countries (in addition to the European Union as a whole) are Argentina, Australia, Brazil, Canada, China, France, Germany, India, Indonesia, Italy, Japan, Mexico, Republic of Korea, Russia, Saudi Arabia, South Africa, Turkey, the UK and the USA.

2 From Emerging to Emerged

1. Angus Maddison, *The World Economy: Historical Statistics*, OECD Development Centre, 2004.

3 BRIC by BRIC

1. Jonathan Wheatley, 'Lunch with the FT: Fernando Henrique Cardoso', *Financial Times*, 24 September 2010.
2. C. J. Chivers, 'Putin Calls for Steps to End Drop in Population', *New York Times*, 10 May 2006.
3. Murray Feshbach, *Russia's Health and Demographic Crises: Policy Implications and Consequences*, Chemical & Biological Arms Control Institute, 2003.
4. Michael Schwirtz, 'Russia Cites Progress on Fertility', *New York Times*, 19 July 2007.
5. Jim O'Neill and Tushar Poddar, 'Ten Things for India to Achieve Its 2050 Potential', Goldman Sachs Global Economics Paper No. 169, June 2008.
6. Quoted in David Barboza, 'Contrarian Investor Sees Economic Crash in China', *New York Times*, 7 January 2010.
7. Jamil Anderlini, 'China's Political Anniversary: A Long Cycle Nears its End', *Financial Times*, 1 July 2011.

4 The New Growth Markets

1. Dominic Wilson and Anna Stupnytska, 'The N-11: More Than an Acronym', Goldman Sachs Global Economics Paper No.153, March 2007.
2. Jim O'Neill, Anna Stupnytska and James Wrisdale, 'It is Time to Re-define Emerging Markets', Goldman Sachs Asset Management Strategy Series, 31 January 2011.

5 Are There Enough Resources?

1. Jim O'Neill, Roopa Purushothaman and Themistoklis Fiotakis, 'The BRICs and Global Markets: Crude, Cars and Capital', Goldman Sachs Global Economics Paper No. 118, October 2004.
2. Jim O'Neill, 'Can the G7 Afford the BRICs Dreams to Come True?', Goldman Sachs Global Economics Paper No. 119, November 2004; Jim O'Neill and Anna Stupnytska, 'The Long-Term Outlook for the BRICs and N-11 Post Crisis', Goldman Sachs Global Economics Paper No.192, December 2009.
3. Reuters citing Xinhua News Agency report quoting the State Council, 26 November 2009.
4. Gordon Conway, 'Beijing Seeks a Head Start in the Race to Go Green', *Financial Times*, 11 November 2009.

6 Consumption

1. Jim O'Neill and Anna Stupnytska, 'The Rise of the BRICs and N-11 Consumer', Goldman Sachs Asset Management Strategy Series, 3 December 2010.

7 New Allies Ahead

1. 'Made in the USA, Again: Manufacturing is Expected to Return to America as China's Rising Labor Costs Erase Most Savings from Offshoring', Boston Consulting Group Press Release, 5 May 2011, available at www.bcg.com/media/PressReleaseDetails.aspx?id=tcm: 12-75973.

8 A New World Order

1. Jim O'Neill, and Robert Hormats, 'The G-8: Time for a Change', Goldman Sachs Global Economics Paper No. 112, 2004.

2. Edwin M. Truman, 'Implications of Structural Changes in the Global Economy for Its Management', Paper delivered at the World Economic Forum – Reinventing Bretton Woods Committee Roundtable on Global Savings and Investments Patterns and the Changing Structure of the World Economy, Adelaide, Australia, 18–19 March, 2006.

9 Invest and Prosper

1. Timothy Moe, Caesar Maasry and Richard Tang, 'EM Equity in Two Decades: A Changing Landscape', Goldman Sachs Global Economics Paper No. 204, September 2010.

2. Francesco Garzarelli, Sandra Lawson, Michael Vaknin, Zhong Sheng and TengTeng Xu, 'Bonding the BRICs: The Ascent of China's Debt Capital Market', Goldman Sachs Global Economics Paper No. 149, November 2006.

3. Francesco Garzarelli, Sandra Lawson, Tushar Poddar and Pragyan Deb, 'India – Bonding the BRICs: A Big Chance for India's Debt Capital Market', Goldman Sachs Global Economics Paper No. 161, November 2007.

Index

Page numbers in **bold** refer to tables.

PHILIP DELVES BROUGHTON

WHAT THEY TEACH YOU AT HARVARD BUSINESS SCHOOL

What *do* they teach you at Harvard Business School?

Graduates of Harvard Business School run many of the world's biggest and most influential banks, companies and countries. But what kind of person does it take to succeed at HBS? And would you want to be one of them?

For anyone who has ever wondered what goes on behind Harvard Business School's hallowed walls, Philip Delves Broughton's hilarious and enlightening account of his experiences on its prestigious MBA programme provides an extraordinary glimpse into a world of case-study conundrums, guest lectures, *Apprentice*-style tasks, booze luging, burn-outs and high flyers.

And with HBS alumni heading the very global governments, financial institutions and FTSE 500 companies whose reckless love of deregulation and debt got us into so much trouble, Delves Broughton discovers where HBS really adds value – and where it falls disturbingly short.

'Delves Broughton captures an essence of HBS that is part cult, part psychological morass, part hothouse . . . His book is invaluable. Quite brilliant'
Simon Heffer, *Literary Review*

'A funny and revealing insider's view . . . his fascination is infectious' *Sunday Times*

'A particularly absorbing and entertaining read' *Financial Times*

'Horrifying and very funny . . . An excellent book' *Wall Street Journal*

GREGORY ZUCKERMAN

THE GREATEST TRADE EVER

Autumn 2008. The world's finances collapse – but one man makes a killing.

John Paulson, a softly spoken hedge-fund manager who still took the bus to work, seemed unlikely to stake his career on one big gamble. But he did – and *The Greatest Trade Ever* is the story of how he realised that the sub-prime housing bubble was going to burst, making $15 billion for his fund and more than $4 billion for himself in a single year. It's a tale of folly and wizardry, individual brilliance versus institutional stupidity.

John Paulson made the biggest winning bet in history. And this tells how he did it.

'Simply terrific. Easily the best of the post-crash financial books' Malcolm Gladwell

'The definitive account of a sensational trade' Michael Lewis, author of *Liar's Poker*

'Extraordinary, excellent' *Observer*

'A great page-turner and a great illuminator of the market's crash' John Helyar, author of *Barbarians at the Gate*

'A must-read for anyone fascinated by financial madness' *Mail on Sunday*

'A forensic, read-in-one-sitting book' *Sunday Times*

RICHARD L. BRANDT

ONE CLICK: Jeff Bezos and the Rise of Amazon.com

Amazon's business model is deceptively simple: make online shopping so easy that customers won't think twice. It can be summed up by that button on every page: 'Buy now with one click'.

Why has Amazon been so successful? Much of it hinges on Jeff Bezos, the CEO and founder, whose unique character and ruthless business sense have driven Amazon relentlessly forward.

Through interviews with Amazon employees and competitors, *One Click* charts Bezos's rise from computer nerd to world-changing entrepreneur. It reveals how he makes decisions and where he will take Amazon next.

Amazon is a case study in how to reinvent an entire industry. It is one that anyone in business ignores at their peril.

'Richard Brandt compellingly profiles one of the great internet executives of the era' Stephen Leeb, author of *The Oil Factor* and *Red Alert*

'Meticulously researched and with breathless, pithy commentary. If you want to understand the Bezos phenomenon, this is an easy and efficient way to do it - just like shopping on Amazon.' *Management Today*

RON ADNER

THE WIDE LENS

Do you own a Sony e-reader? Use Office 2007? Drive on Michelin's run-flat tyres? Probably not. All three are examples of great innovations which tanked at launch through no fault of their own.

Innovation is the single most important subject for companies seeking profitable growth. Endless surveys and research try to help businesses produce game-changing new products, services or approaches. But the majority of innovation still fails. External factors wreck companies' carefully constructed plans and kill off a new product or service before it can realise its potential.

No-one knows how to avoid potential obstacles better than expert business strategist Ron Adner, and in *The Wide Lens* he draws lessons from industries including technology, publishing and healthcare to show how only companies who understand the pitfalls that can kill off great ideas before they happen can hope to make innovation work.

AARON SCHAPIRO

USERS NOT CUSTOMERS: Who Really Determines the Success of Your Business

Boardroom conversations are adapting to a new and brutal reality; there is no such thing as an offline business. And if you don't embrace digital, you'll be out of business altogether.

Blockbuster, AOL, Yahoo and Borders were all unstoppable, but they didn't see the new economic order coming. Google, Facebook, Groupon and Twitter barely existed at the turn of the millennium, but are now rocketing ahead.

Aaron Shapiro is CEO of HUGE, the leading digital agency which builds and operates websites that handle 150 million users a month and bring in $1.2 billion annually for their clients. That's the GDP of a small country. He thinks constantly about the most pressing issue in business today: how can businesses can use digital to thrive?

Shapiro has studied what the businesses succeeding today have in common, and in Users, Not Customers, he teaches us to recognise that it's not just customers who interact with the digital version of our organisations.

The businesses who are now roaring ahead put the interests and the digital experience of all of their users - employees, business partners, media and anyone else who interacts with you through digital channels - ahead of everything else, including their paying customers.

In a world were we are all users you have a choice: you can be sure that people are using your digital ecosystem, or you can be irrelevant.

'Aaron Shapiro wants to take over the world' *Gavin O'Malley*

'A must-read for anyone seeking to integrate digital experiences with their products and services' Ramon Casadesus-Masanell, Harvard Business School